the Culinary Mistress

a love affair with food

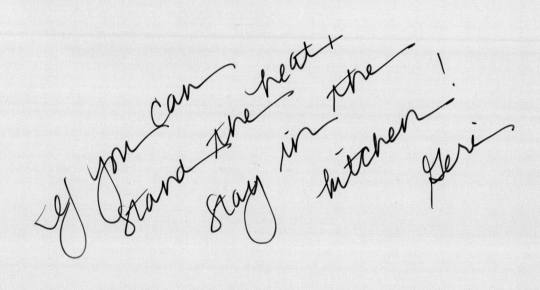

If you can stand the heat + stay in the kitchen!
Geri

Published in Minneapolis, Minnesota by Huntley Wolf, Inc.

Huntley Wolf, Inc. titles may be purchased for educational, business, fund-raising or sales promotion use. For information, please email books@huntleywolf.com.

Printed in the United States of America.

Design by d iDee design.

ISBN 978-0-9832294-0-7

This book is dedicated to chefs who nourish our bodies and feed our souls.

"One cannot think well, love well, sleep well,
if one has not dined well."

- Virginia Woolf

Acknowledgements

It goes without saying that this book would not have happened without the talent and generosity of the chefs contained in the book. Without hesitation they said "yes" and participated with enthusiasm and humility. Chefs, you inspire me every day.

Thank you to Kiersa Notz for the endless hours designing and laying out the book. Much of the credit of the beauty of the book goes to Kiersa. You can accomplish anything you want to in life if you surround yourself with the right people, which is so true in this case. I am grateful that you are a dream maker and a dream giver.

Andrew Zimmern, appreciation goes to you for taking time out of your globe-trotting, testicle and brain-eating schedule to write the forward to the book. The book wouldn't have been complete without it.

To all of those who contributed to the publishing of this book… in both the small ways and the big ways… thank you for helping cross a life-long goal off my list. And thank you for saying "Yes, you're nuts to try to get this done in seven weeks, but do it anyway."

Any errors in the book are mine and mine alone.

As a three-year-old Korean adoptee, I arrived in America at a mere 20 pounds suffering from malnutrition. I remember hearing the comment that if you gave a piece of fish to any of the three adopted children in our family, there wouldn't be a speck of flesh left on the bones.

I haven't stopped eating since.

Growing up on a farm with access to the freshest produce and meat, I learned how to butcher chickens and milk goats and harvest honey — which in turn gave me a true appreciation of food.

In my early twenties, I was set up on a blind date. For our first meeting, the man cooked dinner — including lobster bisque.

It was love. For the man and his soup.

I became ferociously interested in chefs, food and restaurants. An addiction to the Food Network led to a surprise birthday trip to Philadelphia for dinner at then-celebrity chef Philippe Chin's restaurant, Chanterelles.

It was the first time I'd ever heard or sampled French Vietnamese cuisine and my initiation to tasting menus. Tasting menus are developed to expertly pronounce the harmony of certain flavors and textures.

Close to a hundred tasting menus later, I've become a chef groupie. I don't have crushes on movie stars, professional athletes or musicians. No, I have crushes on chefs. Fortunately, they don't seem to mind me stalking them in their restaurants.

The idea of writing a book about chefs was triggered from a message I received from Chef Asher Miller upon finding out I was ill. "What can I do for you? Can I send you some food?"

As I ate the pho he had sent, I felt a deep sense of comfort that I could never fully explain. As long as I can eat, I'll be okay.

Through their recipes and stories, I hope you get to know these chefs as the amazing people and artists that they are.

Incredibly passionate.

Incredibly gifted.

Incredibly generous.

It becomes obvious after spending time — or even cooking with them as I've been lucky enough to do — with chefs that cooking and restaurants are the other women in their lives. *The Culinary Mistress, a Love Affair with Food* was written to tell the stories about these chefs and their love of food. You will notice that this is not a typical cookbook, as each recipe is written in the respective chefs' voice.

Chefs give their heart and soul to their food as it is a way to touch people at the most basic level and many times in the most intricate way. Overwhelmingly generous, they give of their time and talent to the community's numerous charity events.

Every time I dine in a restaurant, I remember that someone put a little of themselves into that plate of food.

I appreciate it. I hope you do, too.

Geri Wolf

The book you hold in your hands is titled *The Culinary Mistress, a Love Affair with Food*, and Geri Wolf calls it a collection of recipes from the top chefs in the Twin Cities, but more importantly *The Culinary Mistress* is about the stories these chefs share with us, stories that yes indeed make the food taste better. The Mistress is not Geri. Sorry to disappoint. The Mistress is the muse at work in the lives of these amazing chefs, the food itself. And where there is a mistress there is passion. And in passion, great tales… impossible opportunity leading to amazing creative potential and for me, the difference between like and love.

Love and passion? Well, yes, the recipes are superb, guaranteed to provide you with years and years of great cooking but the book's strength is capturing those moments we all have as professionals, that moment when you fall in love with food and kick-start a passion for cooking. So rather than set out to document and produce the dull bio driven blurb, Geri sought to lay out the story about the chefs as people, as she knows them, and that personal thought line is what separates this wonderful book from the rest of the pack. What comes from the heart, reaches the heart and the fact that the American Brain Tumor Association is receiving a portion of the proceeds is more than just heartfelt, its at the core of who Geri is as a human being. Her story completes this love letter to a group of chefs who make this city one of the country's great food communities.

Seemingly, Geri's favorite part of the book are the "Amuse Bouche" contributions. Did you know that Erik Anderson managed rock bands for eight years? Or that Asher Miller plays violin? Or that Adrienne Odom has a vast toy collection, which includes over 1000 Matchbox cars? That one makes me jealous. Or that Steven Brown got kicked out of first grade? You will have to find out why for yourself. Geri loves this stuff, and she asked me to share some little known facts about myself. So Geri, thanks for asking me to contribute a few words about my favorite subject… Me.

I am a late nineteenth century history geek who thought he would teach art history. My college thesis was for two departments and chronicled our obsession with pictures in post Civil War America. I collect 19th century maps and prints. I am an avid hunter. I speak passable French. I am obsessed with swimming in oceans and that's why I swam into San Francisco Bay when it was 54 degrees Fahrenheit wearing only a Speedo (swim club rules!). I eat cereal late at night when hungry, I grow tomatoes, I own way too many cameras and do nothing with them. If the TV career implodes I want to run for public office.

Thanks Geri. Glad I got that off my chest.

Andrew Zimmern is the James Beard award-winning host, co-creator and consulting producer of Bizarre Foods with Andrew Zimmern, author of *The Bizarre Truth* and is a contributing editor and columnist with *Mpls-St Paul Magazine* and *Delta Sky Magazine*. For more information, visit www.AndrewZimmern.com.

Erik Anderson | Chef de Cuisine, Sea Change

Although Chef Erik Anderson spent much of his teenage years in the kitchen, it was not in front of a stove. At his parents' Aurora, Illinois restaurant, he was the master of the dishwasher rather than a sauté pan. However, like his Drake Hotel sous chef father, Anderson discovered he enjoyed cooking dishes rather than washing dishes.

Taking a break from the restaurant world for several years, Anderson always felt the tug to return to the kitchen. And some of the kitchens he has worked in are legendary — as in an intense time at French Laundry with the perfection-obsessed Thomas Keller and a month-long stint at Alinea in Chicago.

It was during his tenure at Auriga under the award-winning Doug Flicker, that Anderson caught the eye of Tim McKee. Like McKee, Anderson spends his time in and out of the kitchen reading about cooking methods and perusing food photography, including books *Under Pressure: Cooking Sous Vide, French Laundry, Alinea, White Heat* and *Ma Gastronomie*.

As McKee was contemplating the concept of Sea Change, a sustainable-seafood restaurant, he immediately thought of Anderson. Anderson's experience with French Laundry and Alinea, restaurants known for their high pressure, consistently precise execution was just what the restaurant at the Guthrie Theater needed. Getting crushed with diners before and after performances does little to rattle Anderson.

Anderson and McKee collaborated during the opening of Sea Change at The Guthrie, but once it was open, McKee passed along the artistic license to Anderson. And artist, he is.

While many chefs may name a knife as their favorite tool in the kitchen, spoons hold a special affinity to Anderson. With his coveted spoons acting as brushes and the plate as a canvas, Anderson mimics a painter while plating his dishes.

Langoustines in Brick with Tomato Horseradish and Lemon

Serves 12

12	langoustines, black tail vein removed
1/2 teaspoon	*preserved lemon brunoise (1/8" dice)
4 sheets	**brick dough
3	egg yolks
1 tablespoon	water
2 tablespoons	tomato marmalade
1 tablespoon	horseradish emulsion
1	parsley leaf for garnish
3	lemon zest, thin threads
	Maldon sea salt
	black pepper

TOMATO MARMALADE

750 grams	San Marzano tomatoes, ***hacher, no seeds
50 grams	sugar
200 grams	glucose
5 grams	citric acid
27 grams	pectin
275 grams	tomato water
5 grams	fleur de sel

Cook tomato water to almost au sec (nearly dry). Add tomato and salt and cook 2 minutes. Add glucose and sugar and cook another 2 minutes. Add pectin (sprinkle evenly to ensure no lumps form) and citric acid and cook for 3 minutes, then lay out on a sheet pan to cool.

(continued)

HORSERADISH EMULSION

150 grams	fresh horseradish, grated
1/2 cup	rice wine vinegar
4 cloves	garlic, chopped
1	medium shallot, chopped
1 teaspoon	whole grain mustard
1 tablespoon	****wasabi oil
	salt to taste
3 grams	*****xanthan gum
1/2 quart	canola oil

In a vita prep or food processor, blend all of the ingredients except the canola oil. Once blended, slowly add the canola oil to emulsify.

LANGOUSTINES

Pulse cleaned langoustine tails in a food processor 3 or 4 times. They should still have some texture and not be perfectly smooth. Add brunoise of preserved lemon and season with kosher salt. Place in a pastry bag.

Lay out 1/2 sheet of brick dough and brush with egg yolk and water mixture. Pipe out a line of the langoustine mixture onto the dough and roll to form a cylinder. Chill.

Fry at 350° until golden brown. Immediately after coming out of fryer, season with salt and drain on a paper towel.

TO ASSEMBLE

Place a dollop of tomato marmalade in a small bowl. Add a smaller dollop of horseradish cream in the center. Place a crispy langoustine in the bowl, off to one side. Garnish with lemon zest, Maldon salt, cracked black pepper and parsley.

recipe notes

*Preserved lemon may be purchased online at www.zamourispices.com.

**Brick dough may be purchased at www.levillage.com.

***Hacher is a French term for chopping, just past a minced stage.

****Wasabi oil may be purchased at www.greatciao.com.

*****Xanthan gum is an emulsifier, and is available at many co-ops, or online at www.bobsredmill.com.

FOIE GRAS CURE

14 grams	kosher salt
6 grams	pink salt
2 grams	white pepper
2 grams	sugar

Combine all ingredients. Reserve.

BLACK TRUFFLE PURÉE

500 grams	whole black truffle
150 grams	hen of the woods mushrooms
100 grams	Yukon gold potato, peeled and diced small
500 grams	truffle juice
	truffle oil, sherry vinegar to taste and salt to taste

Combine all ingredients and bring to a simmer. Purée until smooth and adjust seasoning with truffle oil, salt and sherry vinegar.

PICKLED RAMP BULBS

2	ramp bulbs
1 part	sugar
1 part	vinegar
1 part	water

Bring liquid to a boil and pour over ramp bulbs. Pickle ramps for at least 24 hours.

(continued)

amuse bouche

Chef Erik Anderson managed rock bands for eight years, traveling throughout Asia and Europe.

FOIE GRAS

500 grams	foie gras, grade A
14 grams	foie gras cure
1	loaf of brioche, 12 x 4 x 3"

Soak 1 lobe of foie gras in milk for 24 hours. Remove lobe from the milk and let come to room temperature. Devein and trim away any discoloration from the lobe and allow to chill.

Cut foie gras into 1" dice and add foie gras cure. *Cryovack on 10 and allow to cure for 24 hours.

Poach foie gras for 90 seconds, then remove from bag. Pass through a tamis (strainer), then place foie gras in a pastry bag.

Cut loaf of brioche in half. Wrap tightly in plastic wrap and freeze for 24 hours. When frozen, drill a 1 ½" hole through the center of each half. Pipe foie gras into the hole and re-wrap brioche with plastic wrap. Chill until ready to assemble.

TO SERVE

2	pickled ramp bulbs
	black truffle purée
3 grams	Poor Rock Abbey lime marmalade
3	petite orchids
	chive tips
2	red radishes, sliced
2	watermelon radishes, sliced

Slice a 1" thick piece of brioche filled with foie gras and toast lightly.

Garnish with ramp bulbs, black truffle purée, lime marmalade, petite orchids, chive tips and both radishes.

recipe notes

Many of the ingredients called for in this recipe including foie gras, truffles and hen of the woods mushrooms may be found online at www.gourmetfoodstore.com.

*Cryovacking is an industry term for a cooking technique in which food is placed in a plastic bag, vacuum-packed, and then cooked slowly in warm water. The pressure of the packing process is used to infuse flavors into ingredients. In lieu of the cryovack, wrap tightly in plastic wrap.

Maple Thyme Custard

Serves 12

1 cup	heavy cream
1 cup	whole milk
1/4 cup	Blis maple syrup (may substitute any good-quality pure maple syrup)
2 sprigs	fresh thyme
2	egg yolks
2	whole eggs
	truffle oil to taste
	pine extract to taste
12	egg shells
12	*bacon chips

In a medium saucepan, mix heavy cream and milk with maple syrup bring to a boil. Reduce to a simmer for 10 minutes, add the thyme sprigs and let steep for 15 minutes in a warm place.

Remove the thyme sprigs from cream mixture. Whisk the egg yolks and whole eggs together, then temper into the custard base. (To temper, add a small amount of the warm cream mixture to the cold eggs, then add the warmed eggs into the cream. This warms them a bit so they incorporate into the cream instead of cooking.) Add truffle oil and pine extract to taste.

Fill hollowed out egg shells 3/4 of the way with custard and bake in a 300° oven until set. Begin checking for doneness after 20 minutes or so.

Garnish with a bacon chip and fresh thyme leaves.

amuse bouche

Chef Erik Anderson has dined at Nobu London five times. This is five times more often than the average person.

Steven Brown | Executive Chef, Tilia

Tarragon is Chef Steven Brown's favorite ingredient. It is spicy and distinctive, which could also describe Brown himself. Spend any time with the tall, lanky chef and it becomes apparent that he has a quick wit backed by a well-read mind.

As a child, he loved to stay home with his mother looking at Betty Crocker cookbooks. While many pre-teen boys might want a new bike, Brown was pleased to receive a Frydaddy for this eighth-grade graduation present. He used the Frydaddy to make donuts. Lots and lots of donuts.

While his cooking and the equipment he uses may now be a bit more sophisticated, it is the same passion that is evident in the dishes he creates.

Unwittingly, the first time he cooked for a woman he wanted to impress, he made cioppino. She ate the fish stew without telling him she was allergic to garlic. But his effort paid off as she eventually married him anyway.

After an extensive career cooking for other people, Brown is finally at the helm of his own kitchen. His intimate Linden Hills eatery, Tilia (the botanical name for the Linden tree), is the first restaurant that Brown has an ownership stake. While every aspect of the restaurant reflects Brown's taste, it is the menu that reflects his witty, yet approachable personality.

Brown may be best known for creating dishes with components that shouldn't make sense together, but somehow work — and work well. What comes through dish after dish is his respect for the ingredients, the responsibility of knowing where they come from and allowing their natural flavors shine through.

While Brown's food may seem to be intellectual, his philosophy has always been very simple.

Good food tastes good.

1/4 cup	pecan or walnut pieces
1 tablespoon	olive oil
	a few thyme leaves
	kosher salt, brown sugar, cayenne
1/2 pound	brussels sprouts
3 tablespoons	bacon fat, divided
4 ounces	chicken stock, unsalted
2 tablespoons	butter
1/2	lemon, center ribs and seeds removed
	black truffle oil (optional)
4 slices	smoked bacon, such as Nueske's, diced, rendered and reserved (use more if you like!)

Fry the pecans in a little olive oil. When brown and fragrant, add the thyme, give it a few tosses, then remove the nuts with a slotted spoon to a paper towel. Transfer again to a small bowl and while still warm toss with brown sugar, salt and cayenne. Reserve.

Bring a large pot of heavily salted water to a boil. Cut the brussels sprouts in half and peel the bright green outer leaves. Reserve both separately.

Blanch the brussels sprouts for 2 minutes until bright green and tender. Drain, shock in ice water, drain again and reserve.

in a large sauté pan, melt 2 tablespoons of the bacon fat over low heat and add the reserved outer leaves of brussels sprouts, taking care not to burn, cool slowly, turning occasionally until leaves become quite crisp. Remove to a paper towel and season with a little salt and fresh cracked black pepper. Reserve.

Heat a sauté pan over medium-high heat and swirl in remaining bacon fat. When hot, add the halved sprouts, cut side down, to fill the pan (you may have to do this in batches). Cook until brown and caramelized, then add the chicken stock and reduce liquid to a scant amount. Reduce heat and add butter to make a sauce. Squeeze half a lemon over the brussels sprouts and add truffle oil, if using. Toss in bacon and nuts. Taste and adjust seasoning. Serve immediately.

amuse bouche

Chef Steven Brown would be a furniture designer if he wasn't a chef.

1 ½-2 pounds	pork tenderloin, silver skin removed
4	allspice berries
4	juniper berries
12	tellicherry peppercorns
3 sprigs	fresh thyme
1	scallion, sliced into rounds
3	bay leaves
	kosher salt
2-3 tablespoons	unsalted butter at room temperature
1 sprig	fresh thyme
2 cloves	garlic, unpeeled
1	shallot, finely minced
2 tablespoons	parsley, finely chopped
	coarse sea salt, such as Maldon, for garnish

Clean the tenderloin and set aside on a sheet of butcher paper large enough to wrap the meat completely.

Toast the allspice, juniper and peppercorns in a small sauté pan over medium heat until fragrant and they release their oils. Cool and coarsely grind in mortar and pestle or spice grinder. Reserve. Pick the thyme leaves off the stem and crush the bay leaves in your fingers then add that to the mixture.

Measure 1 ½ teaspoons of kosher salt per pound of meat. (For a 2 pound tenderloin use 1 tablespoon of salt.) Mix the reserved spices with the salt and add the scallions. Using the butcher paper to keep the salt and meat together, sprinkle the salt mixture over the meat, taking care to distribute more where the meat is thickest. Fold and twist the butcher paper to make a loose package and refrigerate for 4 hours or up to overnight.

Preheat oven to 350°. Remove meat package from refrigerator, open the paper and pat dry with a paper towel and transfer to a small sheet pan or plate. Discard the paper. Heat a sauté pan over medium-high heat and add a small amount of oil to coat the pan. Add the meat and rotate to brown, then transfer in pan to oven and cook for 6 to 8 minutes until medium-rare. Remove from oven and return to medium heat on the stove. Add the butter, thyme and garlic, then using a large spoon, baste meat until butter browns, coating the meat with the browned solids from the butter. Taking care not to burn the shallots, add them in the last minute to brown in the butter. Continue basting the meat. When the shallots are crisp, add the parsley and baste again, coating the meat with the shallots and parsley. Remove from heat, discarding the butter, garlic and thyme sprig and place pork onto a plate lined with a paper towel to rest for 5 minutes.

Slice and serve with a sprinkle of sea salt if desired and maple apple cider sauce.

Maple Apple Cider Sauce

4 ounces	apple cider
2 ounces	maple syrup
2 ounces	cider vinegar
2 ounces	pork jus or veal demi-glace
1	shallot, finely minced
1-2 tablespoons	butter, cut into chunks

Combine the cider, syrup and vinegar. Stir to dissolve the syrup. Reserve.

In a small pot over medium heat, sweat the shallots in a little oil or butter. Increase heat, add the cider mix and reduce by 2/3, then add pork jus or veal demi-glace. Reduce to approximately 1/4 cup, turn heat to low and swirl in butter, taking care not to break the sauce.

Serve immediately.

amuse bouche

Chef Steven Brown was kicked out of first grade for looking up his teacher's skirt.

"Sex is good, but not as good as fresh, sweet corn."

- Garrison Keillor

Chris Damskey | Chef de Cuisine,
Market by Jean Georges | W Boston

Pudding held a special fascination for Chef Chris Damskey when he was nine. Whenever his parents were away, he would spend hours in the kitchen making boxed pudding.

After mastering pudding out of a box, Damskey began experimenting with pudding from scratch, making his siblings taste-test his creations.

Don't judge the chef on his pistachio pudding with red food coloring. Granted, it looked like a poinsettia gone terribly wrong, but great chefs are made while experimenting in the kitchen.

Starting at a very young age, every Sunday was spent with his grandmother cooking Sunday night's family supper. Damskey's favorite childhood memories are filled with the hours his grandmother would spend with him teaching him how to cook.

While Damskey is now living and cooking in Boston at Market by Jean-Georges in the W Hotel, he left his culinary imprint on Minneapolis during his tenure as chef de cuisine of the now-closed Chambers Kitchen.

Working under restaurateur Jean-Georges Vongerichten keeps Damskey challenged to offer exceptional, yet attainable fine dining experiences. In a high profile foodie city like Boston, Market by Jean-Georges fits right into the environment.

The restaurant's philosophy puts an emphasis on fresh, locally-sourced ingredients and a menu offering comfort and creativity.

A lot like grandma's philosophy.

CARROTS

2 pounds	organic carrots, peeled and thinly sliced
5 ¼ cups	distilled water, cold
2 ounces	granulated sugar
1 ounce	kosher salt

Combine above in a pot and bring to a fast boil, covered with a lid. Remove from heat and add:

14 ounces	carrot, peeled and thinly sliced
5 ounces	parsnip, peeled and thinly sliced

Mix ingredients well, and allow to cool covered at room temperature. Place in a blender and purée until completely smooth. Transfer to a fine mesh strainer lined with a coffee filter and allow to filter overnight in the fridge. You should have 35 ounces of carrot broth. Season with:

1 tablespoon	sugar
1 teaspoon	kosher salt

FARRO

3 ounces	farro, toasted until golden and nutty
2 quarts	distilled water, cold
2 tablespoons	kosher salt
	herb sachet (½ ounce rosemary and ½ ounce thyme, broken, plus 1 ounce lemon peel, with no pith — placed in a cheesecloth)

Rinse toasted farro 2 to 3 times, combine with water and cook until farro is completely tender. Remove from heat and add herb sachet and salt, then cool in a flat pan in the cooking liquid.

TO SERVE

4 ounces	carrot broth, heated to simmer
1 tablespoon	farro, heaping, heated in a little cooking liquid
	French breakfast radish, thinly sliced, seasoned with salt, lemon juice and minced tarragon
	yellow celery leaves

Arrange farro in the bottom of a bowl and scatter seasoned radish slices and yellow celery leaves on top of farro. Heat soup to a simmer (do not boil). Pour on top of farro for tableside presentation.

Serves 8

	strawberries (small summer berries are best — 6 to 7 per person)
	strawberry syrup
	black pepper, cracked
16 ounces	feta cheese (Egyptian or French feta is best, and may be found at Midtown Market or Bill's Imported Foods)
	arugula
	fresh basil
	good quality olive oil
	crystallized wasabi
	fleur de sel (sea salt)

Use the ripest local strawberries available. Wash strawberries well and carefully cut the stem end, then the other side (save the non-stem side). Arrange in an even layer by size on parchment and reserve at room temperature.

(continued)

amuse bouche

Chef Chris Damskey holds a second degree black belt in Tae Kwon Do.

STRAWBERRY SYRUP

1 pound	strawberry scraps (supplement with whole strawberries, stemmed and thinly sliced)
2 ounces	granulated sugar
1 teaspoon	kosher salt

Place above in a bowl and cover tightly with saran wrap. Place over a double boiler and cook over medium heat, allowing the strawberries to steam until they are cooked to a complete mush. Transfer to a blender and process until completely smooth. Reserve.

CRYSTALLIZED WASABI

1 ounce	organic wasabi powder
1 tablespoon	water
1 ½ ounces	sugar

Mix wasabi and water to form a smooth paste and let stand 15 minutes. Work the sugar into the paste little by little with a spatula until completely absorbed by the wasabi — it should look like clumpy wet sand. Let dry at room temperature at least 1 hour prior to serving.

TO SERVE

Pack a 4 ½" ring mold as tightly as possible with the strawberries and drizzle liberally with strawberry syrup, and add fresh cracked black pepper. Crumble feta liberally on top, then layer the wild arugula over the cheese. Scatter a chiffonade of basil over the arugula and drizzle with olive oil. Sprinkle with wasabi candy and finish with a sprinkle of fleur de sel.

amuse bouche

Chef Chris Damskey sports 13 tattoos — the largest being a yellow fin tuna swimming in the ocean.

Serves 4-6

1	whole beef short rib plate (3 bones-in), about 3 ½ pounds average
	kosher salt to season
2	garlic heads, cut in half
5 ounces	large shitake mushrooms, stems and all
8 ounces	carrot, peeled and thinly sliced
5	large onions, peeled and diced ½"
1 head	celery, cleaned and diced medium
2 ounces	ginger, peeled and sliced medium thin
1 small sheet	konbu (optional)
1 small bunch	fresh thyme sprigs (roughly one package or 1 ounce)
1 bottle (750 ml)	red wine, reduced to 1 cup
4 ounces	red wine vinegar
2 gallons	hot chicken stock, or just enough to cover

Season ribs with salt and let stand 10 minutes. Combine remaining ingredients in a high sided roasting pan or a dutch oven and cover with 2 sheets of foil. Cook in a 305° oven until ribs are completely tender, about 4 to 5 hours. The meat should have no resistance to the touch and fall off of the bones.

Once cooked, use a spider to carefully remove ribs and transfer to a baking sheet. Carefully slide out bones, then double wrap the beef in saran wrap. Place another baking sheet with a small weight on top to lightly compress the beef, and refrigerate until completely cooled. Once cooled, unwrap and trim off excess fat and portion into perfect square portions. Reserve.

Strain braising liquid through a china cap, then a chinois. Reduce liquid by half over medium heat. Skim off impurities. Reserve.

RED WINE REDUCTION

1 bottle (750 ml)	red wine (malbec or zinfandel)
350 ml	ruby port
5 ounces	red wine vinegar
5 ounces	granulated sugar
1 piece	Chinese star anise, crushed
5	allspice berries, crushed
1	cinnamon stick, crushed
pinch	cumin seeds, toasted

(continued)

Combine all ingredients and reduce to a syrup. When strained there should be approximately 10 ounces of red wine reduction.

RED WINE-MISO

7 ounces	red wine reduction
5 ounces	red miso
1 ounce	red wine vinegar
1 teaspoon	kosher salt
1 teaspoon	ground black peppercorn

Combine all ingredients and purée until smooth.

CARROT PURÉE

1 ½ pounds	organic carrots, peeled and very thinly sliced
8 cups	water
1 tablespoon	kosher salt
2 tablespoons	granulated sugar

Combine above in a pot and bring to a boil. Let boil rapidly until carrots are very tender. Strain through a chinois, then purée until totally smooth.

VEGETABLES

In a large pan over medium heat, add 1 tablespoon of grapeseed oil and lightly caramelize the baby brussels sprouts evenly until just cooked through. Add chanterelles and sear until just cooked. Remove from heat, add fresh thyme and serve immediately with the ribs.

TO SERVE (PER PLATE)

6 ounce portion	short rib
6 ounces	braising liquid mix (2 parts rib jus reduction to 1 part red wine miso glaze), approximately (2-4 ounces per rib)
	carrot purée, warmed through in sauce pan
1 ounce	chanterelles, trimmed and cleaned
2 ½ ounces	baby brussels sprouts, outer leaves trimmed and stems removed
	fresh thyme

Portion ribs and reheat while basting in cooking liquid in oven at 350°, until warmed through and completely glazed with braising liquid mix. Liquid should be concentrated to a glaze consistency and short rib should be shiny and wet.

With a mini offset spatula, place an even stripe of warmed carrot purée from 12 to 6 o'clock. Place glazed short rib in center of stripe, just offset, and garnish with the chanterelles and brussels sprouts to the right of the rib (on the opposite side of the carrot stripe).

Michael DeCamp | Chef de Cuisine, La Belle Vie

If it is possible for someone to have a cooking gene, it would definitely be flowing in Chef Michael DeCamp's blood.

At the age of seventeen, DeCamp started working for D'Amico Cucina Executive Chef Tim McKee. McKee, boss and mentor, nicknamed DeCamp "Young Chef", which was shortened to Y.C.

For eight years, DeCamp worked under McKee's direction off and on, taking a couple of years to work in Chicago. In 2005, he went to work for McKee at the new Minneapolis location of the French Mediterranean La Belle Vie, where he has remained since. Eventually, he was promoted to the position of Chef de Cuisine at La Belle Vie, having earned the trust of his boss and mentor to write menus and run the kitchen.

With numerous restaurant awards comes a lot of responsibility. DeCamp has the ability to channel his boss's cooking style, yet maintain his individual approach to developing menus and cooking. It is their mutual level of trust that enables DeCamp to keep McKee's philosophy intact, while still granting him the freedom to create in the kitchen.

When he seeks inspiration, DeCamp browses through the backpack of cookbooks and food photography. DeCamp loves to experiment with new cooking methods, flavor combinations and ingredients, all of which bring attention focused on him, separate from his mentor.

Spend any time with DeCamp — or follow him on any social media vehicle — and it quickly becomes obvious he thinks about food and cooking all of the time. And one would also think that DeCamp is on a one-man mission to bring foie gras into everyone's regular dining repertoire.

While it is apparent that cooking (and baking) is the "other woman" in the life of the newly married DeCamp, fortunately, cooking is the "other man" in the life of his executive sous chef wife.

Serves 4

POLENTA

1 cup	Anson Mills stone ground yellow cornmeal
4 cups	water
1 pound	Parmesano Reggiano, finely grated on a microplane
1/2 cup	mascarpone
1/4 cup	heavy cream
1/2 cup	butter
1/4 cup	extra virgin olive oil
	salt

In a heavy bottomed pan over high heat, bring the water to a boil. Stir in the cornmeal and cook for about 20 minutes or until the cornmeal is hydrated. Once the cornmeal is fully hydrated, add the Parmesano Reggiano, mascarpone, cream, butter and olive oil, stirring continuously. Season to taste.

RAPINI

extra virgin olive oil

1 bunch	rapini, cleaned
2 tablespoons	red chili flakes
	salt

In a heavy bottomed saucepan heat extra virgin olive oil until nearly smoking. Add the rapini and chili flakes and cook until the thick part of the rapini is tender. Season to taste. Serve in a bowl with polenta, and enjoy.

Butter Lettuce Salad with Herbs

Serves 4

1/4 cup	Champagne vinegar
1/2 cup	extra virgin olive oil
1	large shallot, minced
3 tablespoons	Italian parsley, chopped
1 tablespoon	chives, minced
2 tablespoons	chervil, minced
1 tablespoon	tarragon, minced
2 tablespoons	picked dill
	salt and freshly ground pepper
	red pepper flakes

Mix all ingredients together and set aside.

2 heads	butter lettuce
	vinaigrette

Remove the core from the butter lettuce and peel the leaves apart. Place the leaves in a large bowl and toss with as much vinaigrette as desired. Adjust seasoning to taste, and divide among four plates.

Serves 4

FOR THE PASTA DOUGH

4 cups	*00 flour
2 whole	eggs
6	egg yolks
2 tablespoons	extra virgin olive oil

Make a well in the center of the flour and add the eggs, yolks and olive oil to the center. Stir with a fork until a loose dough starts to come together, then knead the dough for about 15 minutes. Let rest for 30 minutes before rolling.

FILLING

250 grams	butternut squash purée (strained in a cheesecloth overnight, in the refrigerator)
50 grams	ricotta (strained in a cheesecloth overnight, in the refrigerator)
50 grams	Pecorino Romano, grated
50 grams	mascarpone

Mix all ingredients well and set aside in the refrigerator.

SAGE BUTTER

1/4 pound	butter, room temperature
12	large sage leaves

Chiffonade the sage, and mix butter and sage together until well incorporated.

RED WINE REDUCTION

1 bottle (750 ml)	cheap red wine
1/4 cup	sugar

In a heavy bottomed sauce pan, mix the sugar and wine. Reduce until a syrupy consistency is achieved.

(continued)

FRIED SAGE

| 8 | sage leaves |
| 2 cups | oil, for frying |

Heat the oil to 350° and fry the sage until crispy.

EGG WASH

| 1 | brown egg |
| 2 tablespoons | milk |

| 12 | brown eggs, separated (set yolks aside, being careful not to break, reserve whites for another use.) |
| | microgreens |

TO SERVE

Bring a pot of heavily salted water to a boil. Make an egg wash with one whole egg and the milk. Roll the pasta through a pasta machine to its thinnest setting. Place a 2" cutter on the sheet of pasta and place 1/2 cup of the filling in the center of the cutter. Make a well in the center of the filling and place 1 egg yolk in the well. Use the egg wash to paint around the squash. Cover with a sheet of pasta and seal, making sure you get all the air out. Cut out raviolos with a 3" cutter.

Drop the raviolos into the boiling salted water. While they cook, gently melt the sage butter in a pan. When the pasta is ready (about 4-5 minutes), remove from water and toss gently in the sage butter.

To plate, place one raviolo per person on one side of the plate, and make a line with the red wine reduction on the other. Top with a fried sage leaf and microgreens.

The recipe will make a little more than you need, but can be saved as leftovers..

recipe notes

*00 flour is a low protein Italian flour with very fine granules. It may be found at specialty shops and online at www.delcofoods.com. A mix of low-protein cake flour and all-purpose flour can be substituted for the 00 flour called for.

Serves 4

FENNEL SOUBISE

2 tablespoons	extra virgin olive oil
1	yellow onion, diced small
2 pounds	fennel, rough chopped
1/2 cup	white wine
1 cup	whole milk
2 tablespoons	Champagne vinegar
	salt

In a heavy bottomed saucepan over medium heat, heat the olive oil. Just before it starts to smoke, add the onion and sweat until translucent. Add the fennel, stirring often. Once the fennel starts to cook add the white wine, whole milk and champagne vinegar and cook covered until the fennel is soft, adding water if the pan gets too dry. Transfer mixture to a blender and blend on high until smooth. Season with salt and pass through a fine mesh sieve. Reserve.

CARAMELIZED FENNEL

2 tablespoons	butter
1 tablespoon	extra virgin olive oil
2 pounds	fennel, diced medium
	salt and freshly ground black pepper, to taste

In a heavy bottomed saucepan over medium heat, melt the butter and olive oil. Add the fennel, then turn heat to very low and cook, stirring often until a nice golden color is achieved. Transfer to a blender and blend until smooth. Season and reserve.

TRUFFLE SAUCE

1 tablespoon	extra virgin olive oil
2 tablespoons	shallots, minced
2 ounces	canned truffles, drained
1 cup	heavy cream
	salt and freshly ground black pepper, to taste

In a heavy bottomed saucepan over medium heat, sweat the shallots in olive oil. When translucent add the canned truffles and the cream. Cook over low heat, stirring often until the cream has reduced to 1/2 cup. Transfer to a blender and blend until smooth. Do not strain. Season and reserve.

(continued)

SAUTÉED MÂCHE

1 tablespoon	extra virgin olive oil
1 4 ounces	mâche
	salt and freshly ground black pepper, to taste

In a heavy bottomed saucepan over high heat, heat the olive oil. Just before it starts to smoke, add the mâche and cook until wilted. Season, transfer to a cookie sheet and refrigerate to cool.

WHITE ASPARAGUS

12 spears	white asparagus, blanched and shocked
1/4 cup	chicken stock
2 tablespoons	butter
2 tablespoons	extra virgin olive oil
	salt

Peel the outside layer of the white asparagus if it is very fibrous. Cut each asparagus spear in two pieces, starting at the tip and discarding the bottom quarter, creating 24 pieces. Place the asparagus in a saucepan and add chicken stock, butter and olive oil. Season with salt and cook until most of the liquid has evaporated. Set aside.

TO SERVE

	extra virgin olive oil
12	U-10 "dry pack" sea scallops
	fennel soubise
	truffle sauce
	caramelized fennel
	wilted mâche
	white asparagus
4 ounces	fresh mâche
1 head	fennel, shaved on a mandoline
	salt and freshly ground black pepper, to taste
	lemon zest

In a medium saute pan over high heat, heat olive oil. Season scallops on both sides with salt and pepper, and cook until golden brown on both sides. Place scallops on paper towels to absorb any excess moisture.

In the center of each plate add one quarter of the fennel soubise. On the outside of the soubise, place three dots of the truffle sauce. Place three scallops per plate. In the center of the scallops place the caramelized fennel, wilted mâche and six spears of white asparagus. In a small stainless steel bowl, toss the fresh mâche with shaved fennel, extra virgin olive oil, lemon zest, salt and pepper, and place in the center of each plate.

Philip Dorwart | Executive Chef, Create Catering

Working as a cook was the first and only job Chef Philip Dorwart ever loved. He loved it enough to change directions, drop out of college and attend the Culinary Institute of America.

After spending time working in New York, Dorwart returned to Minnesota and went back to work at the kitchen that started it all, Table of Contents, eventually becoming a partner in the award-winning restaurant.

And while there was heartache when Table of Contents closed, it was Dorwart's opportunity to try some different things. Dorwart closed the restaurant with a lot of decisions to make about his future. But he was no longer alone in his decision making. Dorwart's former intern, also a chef, had asked him out on a date at the end of her last shift. Not only had he said yes, he eventually married her.

Dorwart worked as a chef for a handful of restaurants in the following years, but knew he wanted to work for himself again.

While Dorwart loves being a chef, the restaurant lifestyle offered little appeal. With that in mind, the Dorwarts opened a catering company focused on serving sophisticated, relaxed food — reflecting their similar lifestyle.

After opening the catering company, Dorwart purchased a Minnesota farm with a 140 year old barn. Sadly, the barn was crushed during a summer storm, but the farm allows Dorwart to get his hands dirty and keep true to his commitment to offer organic vegetables utilizing sustainable practices in every way he can.

Dorwart continues his culinary education by traveling and trying new cuisine, dining out and reading about food whenever possible. In turn, he is able to share his knowledge on a weekly radio show and magazine blog.

Serves 4 - 8 (makes 16 rolls)

1 pound	ground pork
1	small bag bean thread noodles, soaked in warm water for 20 minutes
2 cups	cabbage, shredded
1 cup	onion, diced
1/2 cup	black fungus, soaked in warm water for 1 hour
2 tablespoons	oyster sauce
2 tablespoons	soy sauce
1 tablespoon	ground ginger
	salt and pepper to taste
1 package	Lumpia style egg roll wrappers

Mix all ingredients together, and sauté a small portion to check taste. Adjust seasonings if necessary. Spoon 2 tablespoons of the mixture onto 1 egg roll wrapper, in a line near the edge. Fold wrapper over mixture and roll the filling into a tube. When you reach the middle of the wrapper, fold the right and left sides of the wrapper in, and finish rolling. Moisten the exposed edge of the wrapper and press gently to seal.

NUOC CHAM

1 cup	fish sauce
1 cup	lime juice
1/2 - 3/4 cups	sugar

Mix all ingredients and stir until sugar is dissolved.

CUCUMBER SALAD

2 cups	cucumbers, julienned
1 package	rice noodles, soaked in boiling water for 7 minutes
1/4 cup	fresh basil
1/4 cup	fresh mint
1/4 cup	cilantro
1/2 cup	carrot, shredded
	nuoc cham for dressing
	sriracha for garnish

Mix all ingredients, dress with nuoc cham and allow to marinate for 15 minutes. Serve egg rolls with salad and sriracha for garnish.

MASCARPONE ICE CREAM

4	large egg yolks
3/4 cup	sugar, plus 2 tablespoons
2 cups	whole milk
1 cup	mascarpone (7 ounces)
1/2 teaspoon	fresh lemon juice
pinch	salt

In a large bowl, using a handheld mixer, beat the egg yolks with 3/4 cup of the sugar at medium-high speed until fluffy, about 3 minutes. In a saucepan, combine the milk with the remaining 2 tablespoons of the sugar and bring to a simmer. Slowly beat the warm milk into the egg yolks at low speed. Scrape the custard into the saucepan. Cook over moderate heat, stirring constantly with a wooden spoon, until thick enough to coat the back of the spoon, about 5 minutes; do not let the custard boil.

Pour the custard into a bowl set in a larger bowl of ice water and whisk in the mascarpone, lemon juice and salt. Let stand until chilled, stirring occasionally, 30 minutes.

Pour the custard into an ice cream maker and freeze according to the manufacturer's instructions. Transfer the mascarpone ice cream to an airtight container and freeze until firm, at least 2 hours.

SEA SALT CARAMEL

1 cup	sugar
1/2 cup	heavy cream
2 tablespoons	unsalted butter
2 pinches	sea salt or smoked sea salt

In a small saucepan, heat sugar on medium-high heat until it becomes amber colored and slightly smoking. Gently stir sugar with a fork when color starts, stirring only once. Remove from heat and whisk in cream, then whisk in butter. Add salt and cool slightly before pouring over ice cream.

amuse bouche

Chef Philip Dorwart's father designed the first sub to air missile.

Serves 10 (20 sliders)

6-8 pounds	oxtail (the larger the cut the better — may substitute brisket or chuck roast)
	salt and pepper to taste
1/2 stick	unsalted butter
2 bottles (750 ml)	dry red wine (inexpensive, but something you would drink)
3	onions, peeled, rough chopped
10 cloves	garlic, rough chopped
2	medium carrots, rough chopped
2 ribs	celery
4 sprigs	fresh thyme
2	bay leaves
4-6 cups	beef or chicken broth (may substitute water)

Season the raw oxtail with salt and pepper. In a large stock pot, melt butter, and sear the oxtail until nicely dark brown (not burned!). Add wine and deglaze the pot, scraping all of the goodies from the bottom. Add remaining ingredients and bring to a boil. Turn heat down to a low simmer, cover and place in a 375° oven for 5-6 hours, or until meat is falling from the bone.

Allow meat to cool in the braising liquid until able to handle. Pick meat from bone, removing fat. Strain braising liquid and reduce by half. Adjust seasoning if necessary.

HORSERADISH SOUR CREAM

1 cup	sour cream
1/4 cup	fresh or prepared horseradish
2 teaspoons	mustard oil
pinch	salt

Mix all ingredients together and reserve.

(continued)

BRIOCHE BUNS (makes 20 buns)

1 cup	warm water
3 tablespoons	warm milk
2 teaspoons	active dry yeast
2 ½ tablespoons	sugar
2	large eggs, divided
3 cups	bread flour
1/3 cup	all-purpose flour
1 ½ teaspoon	salt
2 ½ tablespoons	unsalted butter, softened
	sea salt and caraway for sprinkling

In a bowl, combine 1 cup warm water, milk, yeast and sugar. Let stand until foamy, about 5 minutes. Meanwhile, beat 1 egg.

In a large bowl, whisk flours with salt. Add butter and rub into flour between your fingers, making crumbs. Using a dough scraper, stir in yeast mixture and beaten egg until a dough forms. Scrape dough onto clean counter and knead until smooth and elastic, 8 to 10 minutes — don't skimp on time.

Place dough in bowl and cover with plastic wrap. Let rise in a warm place until doubled, about two hours.

Line a sheet pan with parchment paper. Using dough scraper, divide dough into 20 equal parts. Gently roll each into a ball and arrange 1" apart on baking sheet. Cover loosely with a clean kitchen towel and let buns rise in a warm place for 1-2 hours.

Preheat oven to 400° with rack in center. Beat remaining egg with 1 tablespoon of water and brush on top of buns. Sprinkle with sea salt and caraway seeds. Bake until tops are golden brown, about 12 minutes, rotating sheet pan halfway through baking.

TO PLATE
Toast halved buns. Place 2 ounces of meat on bun, top with a pickle and slather with horseradish sour cream — and serve with a napkin!

"As for butter versus margarine, I trust cows more than chemists."

- Joan Gussow

Vincent Francoual | Executive Chef,
Vincent, A Restaurant

Ten year old Chef Vincent Francoual was undeterred by his first attempt to cook a biscuit, even though it "went very bad." By age eleven, French-born Francoual knew he wanted to be a chef — somewhat motivated by his desire to travel the world. Oh, and the fact he would not have to wear a suit to work.

After cooking his way through France, Italy and Great Britain, Francoual decided to try the United States for a while. His temporary stay in the United States became permanent after meeting his wife at one of the New York restaurants he worked.

During his time in New York, Francoual worked for restaurant greats Eric Ripert of Le Bernardin and Gray Kunz of Lespinasse Restaurant, both leaving a permanent impression on him with their passion and their striking cooking style.

Following a move to Minnesota, Francoual opened his namesake restaurant, Vincent a Restaurant, which quickly became popular among the foodie crowd.

His philosophy is to keep things simple and make sure that the natural flavor of the food shines through. Just ask Twins fans, as his award-winning Vincent Burger is one of the most popular items sold at the new Target Field.

While Francoual has enjoyed seeing cooking and dining evolve, he does note that families do not sit down to eat meals together like they used to. Eating is about sharing and as Francoual says "A meal can be good by yourself, but it can be great if shared."

Francoual believes sharing extends to the kitchen and encourages his team to exchange ideas and knowledge. He is known for collaborating in the kitchen, all with the idea of giving the best he has to offer to his diners.

Serves 10

1 quart	heavy cream, divided
1 ounce	Earl Grey tea
14 ounces	milk chocolate
14 ounces	dark chocolate
7 ounces	sugar
1 ounce	water
9	egg yolks

In a medium pot, bring half of the heavy cream and the earl grey tea to a boil. Remove from heat after it has reached boiling. Let steep for 15 minutes and then strain.

Chop milk and dark chocolate into pieces. Return the cream to a boil and pour the cream over the chocolate to melt. Stir until smooth.

In a separate pot, mix the sugar with 1 ounce of water. Heat mixture until it reaches 250°, then turn heat off. In a mixer, add the egg yolks, then slowly add the sugar syrup. Mix well and let cool completely.

Whip the remainder of the cream, and add the whipped cream to the egg yolk mixture. Stir in the melted chocolate (ganache). Place in a terrine mold and place in freezer for 24 hours to set.

amuse bouche

Chef Vincent Francoual completed his first Ironman in 2010 with a race time of 12 hours and 59 minutes.

Vincent's Favorite Childhood Dessert
Good Vanilla Ice Cream, Warm Chocolate Sauce
Madeleine Cookies

A nonstick mini madeleine pan is needed for this recipe.

Makes 100 mini madeleines

MADELEINE COOKIES

11 ounces	granulated sugar
11 ounces	flour
4 teaspoons	baking powder
1	lemon, zested
1	orange, zested
11 ounces	butter
6	eggs
1/2 ounces	vanilla extract

Preheat oven to 350°. In a large bowl, mix the sugar, flour and baking powder together. Add zested lemon and orange to dry ingredients.

Melt the butter. Let cool for a short time, then add the eggs to the butter, whisking together. Add the butter mixture to the dry ingredients and mix until smooth. Add the vanilla extract and mix until well blended. Let rest for 40 minutes.

Spray madeleine tin with cooking spray and pipe the batter into each of the molds. Bake for 5 minutes or until lightly golden around the edges.

Serve with good vanilla ice cream and warm chocolate sauce.

amuse bouche

Chef Vincent Francoual was one of the main organizers behind "Fork the Fire", a fundraising event to help Heidi's and Blackbird, two restaurants that were burned down in 2010.

Serves 4

BIGARADE SAUCE

1	lemon
1	orange
3 ounces	sugar
1/2 ounce	red wine vinegar
1 teaspoon	cracked peppercorn
1 cup (8 ounces)	*duck stock or veal demi-glace

Zest the lemon and orange and squeeze the juice from the fruit. Reserve.

To make a caramel, in a sauce pan over medium heat, add sugar and just enough water to dissolve the sugar into a liquid. Deglaze the caramel with the vinegar, lemon and orange juice. Reduce by half, then add the stock and zest, and reduce again to consistency that coats the back of a spoon.

DUCK BREAST

4	duck breasts
	salt and pepper to taste

Score the fat of the duck breast with a knife. Season the duck with salt and pepper. Warm a sauté pan over medium heat and add duck breast, fat side down. By doing this you will render the fat and have crispy skin. Once the fat has rendered, flip the duck breast and finish in an oven at 375° for 3 minutes or more, depending on the desired meat temperature.

Serve duck breast with bigarade sauce.

recipe notes

*Duck stock and veal demi-glace are available online at www.dartagnan.com.

Håkan Lundberg | Chef de Cuisine, Cosmos | Graves 601 Hotel

After attending culinary school, Chef Håkan Lundberg went on to cook at a number of top restaurants in his native country of Sweden.

Driven to elevate his craft, Lundberg was encouraged to travel and was told that he must spend some time cooking in America. It seemed as if fate intervened, as a fax from Marcus Samuelsson posted kitchen positions for the ambitious opening of Aquavit in Minneapolis, Minnesota.

Minnesota, known for its Swedish heritage, seemed a natural fit for Aquavit and the young Lundberg. While working under the young wunderkind Samuelsson (who wasn't much older than Lundberg), Lundberg's position served to introduce him to the Minnesota palate.

Deciding to stay in Minnesota after Aquavit closed, Lundberg landed at Cosmos. He found a restaurant that allowed him to showcase his ability to meld art and science. Plating with the touch of an artisan, yet creating dishes utilizing molecular gastronomy techniques keeps his cooking fresh and surprising.

Unwilling to rest on his laurels, Lundberg continues to work on his craft participating in stages at a number of the most respected restaurants in the country. Stages refer to culinary auditions in the kitchen and can be nerve-wracking, especially when the stages are in the kitchens of Alinea or *wd*-50.

Lundberg's pursuit of perfection and willingness to experiment has paid off. Cosmos has won multiple awards under his watchful eye.

Serves 4

ROASTED BEETS

24	mixed baby beets
1/2 cup	blend oil
1/2 cup	water
1/2 cup	mixed herbs
	salt and pepper, to taste

Place all ingredients in an oven safe pan and cover with aluminum foil. Roast at 375° for 1 hour. Make sure beets are cooked all the way through, and peel off beet skins with a paper towel. Refrigerate.

SPICED PECANS

1 cup	pecans
1/2 cup	sugar
1 teaspoon	nutmeg
1 teaspoon	cloves
1 teaspoon	cinnamon

Boil pecans for 10 minutes, then drain. Caramelize the sugar in a sauce pan with a little bit of water. When sugar is dark brown add the boiled pecans and stir with a wooden ladle until all of the pecans are coated with caramelized sugar. Add the spices and stir. Spread out the pecans on a non-stick baking sheet to dry in oven at 200° for 4-6 hours.

DEEP FRIED BEET GREENS

4 large leafs	beet greens
	cornstarch
	salt to taste

Dust the washed beet greens with cornstarch and deep fry in 350° oil until crispy. Let the greens drain on a paper towel and season with salt.

(continued)

PICKLED BEET SHEET

2	red beets, large, peeled
4 tablespoons	white vinegar
8 tablespoons	water
4 tablespoons	sugar
2	bay leafs
2 grams	agar agar
1/2 gram	locust bean gum

Place the peeled red beets in a sauce pan with the vinegar, water, sugar and bay leafs. Simmer for 10 minutes. Strain and reserve the liquid.

Pour 125 grams of the reserved pickling liquid in a sauce pan, add agar agar and locust bean gum and simmer for 90 seconds to activate the agar agar. Strain the liquid onto a flat 12 x 10" baking sheet, and place flat in the refrigerator to set.

TO PLATE

8 tablespoons	chevre
	roasted beets
	spiced pecans
	pickled beet sheet
20 leafs	arugula, washed and dried
	deep fried beet greens

Spread 2 tablespoons of chevre on the center of each of 4 plates. Place 6 each of the different roasted beets on top of the chevre. Roughly chop the spiced pecans and place two random piles on top of the chevre. Cut ribbons of the pickled beet sheet and let fall on top of the beets. Garnish with 5 pieces of arugula and deep fried beet greens.

amuse bouche

Chef Håkan Lundberg plays heavy metal guitar and has a recording studio in his home.

Serves 4

SCALLOPS

8	diver scallops
4 tablespoons	*fennel pollen
	salt and pepper to taste

Clean and rinse the scallops under cold water, and dry on paper towels. Dust with fennel pollen, salt and pepper. Reserve, chilled.

CORN GANACHE

8-10 ears	corn
1/2 cup	cream
1/4 cup	mixed soft herbs, such as tarragon, parsley and chives
1/2	medium onion, diced
5 grams	agar agar
	salt and pepper to taste

Cut the corn from the cobs. Divide corn and ears between 2 sauce pans, and make a corn stock with the ears of corn and just enough water to cover the corn cobs.

In a third sauce pan, simmer the cream and herbs for 5 minutes. Add the diced onions to the corn, then add the corn stock to the cream and cook for 25 minutes.

Strain the herbs from the cream and add the cream mixture to the corn. Simmer for 10 minutes, then place in a vita mixer or blender and process until smooth. Strain through a chinois.

Place 250 grams of corn "soup" in a sauce pan, and simmer with the agar agar for 90 seconds to activate. Chill for 45 minutes, then place the hardened corn "soup" in a vita mixer and purée in to a smooth ganache. Transfer to a pastry bag and keep cold.

(continued)

CHORIZO MOUSSE

8 ounces	chorizo picante (hot)
1/2	medium onion, diced
1/3 cup	cream
1 cup	fish stock
	salt and pepper to taste

Sauté chorizo and onions in sauce pan. Drain half the fat from the chorizo. Add cream and fish stock to the pan and simmer for 20 minutes. Place in vita mixer or blender and mix until smooth. Adjust seasonings. Strain through a chinois and chill.

LENTILS

8-10 tablespoons	black beluga lentils
1 cup	fish stock
1 tablespoon	butter
4 tablespoons	fennel stalks, minced
	salt and pepper to taste

Cook lentils in pot with fish stock until al dente. Add butter and fennel to finish. Season to taste.

TO PLATE

Sear the dusted scallops with butter in medium hot sauté pan, basting with butter as it browns.

Pipe corn ganache on each plate like a snake. Scoop out a nice serving of the chorizo mousse using a hot teaspoon, placing in the middle of the plate on top of the corn ganache. Warm the lentils and place two random piles on the corn "snake". Place the seared scallops on top of the lentils and garnish with fresh nasturtium leafs.

recipe notes

*Fennel pollen is sweet and pungent, with a flavor similar to fennel seed, but more intense. Fennel pollen is available online at www.thespicehouse.com.

Serves 4

FOIE GRAS

1 pound	foie gras, grade A

Clean the foie gras of any veins and fat, and cut into four 1 ounce pieces. Save scraps for the tourchon.

FOIE GRAS TOURCHON

Cure all the foie gras pieces in the curing bag with a mixture of salt, sugar, and pink salt to taste. Seal in vacuum bag or zip lock bag. (Submerge the zip lock bag with the foie gras inside in cold water with the opening above the water surface to press out any air in the bag.) Cure for an hour.

Cook foie gras in a hot water bath at 110° for 10-15 minutes. Strain any fat and reserve for the foie gras powder.

Pass the cooked foie gras through a tami and then thru a chinois (both are fine mesh strainers). Refrigerate for about 10 minutes until firm. Roll into a log shape with cheesecloth, and chill for at least 4 hours.

RAISIN PUDDING

1/2 cup	golden raisins
pinch	turmeric
pinch	saffron
1/2 cup	white wine
1/2 cup	water
1/2 cup	dark raisins
1/2 cup	port wine
1/2 cup	water

Cook golden raisins over medium heat with turmeric, saffron, white wine and water. Reduce by 2/3 and process in vita mixer or blender until smooth.

Cook dark raisins over medium heat with port wine and water. Reduce by 2/3 and process in vita mixer or blender until smooth.

(continued)

GLÖGG SPAGHETTI

250 grams	glögg
3 grams	locust bean gum
7 grams	agar agar

Heat glögg, locust bean gum and agar agar, and simmer for 90 seconds. Suck up the warm liquid into *silicon tubes using a syringe and transfer to ice bath. Fill the syringe with air and force the congealed glögg spaghetti out from the tube.

BRIOCHE CRUMBLES

4 slices	brioche, thinly sliced
	reserved foie gras fat from the tourchon
6 ounces	tapioca maltodextrian (approximately, use as much as is needed)

Spread foie gras fat on the brioche slices. Bake at 350° until bread is completely dry. Transfer to a food processor and process the dry brioche to form crumbles.

Mix the warm fat from the tourchon with tapioca maltodextrian until a powder consistency is achieved. Combine the brioche crumbles and the foie gras fat powder in equal amounts.

TO PLATE

	brioche crumbles
	foie gras tourchon
4 tablespoons	almonds, shaved and toasted
	raisin pudding
	glögg spaghetti
	foie gras

Place brioche crumbles down on center of each plate. Cut two thick slices of the tourchon, then cut in half so you have 4 half moon shaped pieces. Crust the outside of the tourchon with the toasted almonds and place the tourchon on top of the brioche crumble pile. Place random dots of raisin pudding on the plate. Place 2 of the glögg spaghettis on the plate, having them weave in and out of the dish.

In medium hot pan, sear off the four 1 ounce foie gras pieces to medium, and place in the center of the dish. Serve immediately so you can enjoy the hot and cold preparation of the foie gras.

recipe notes

*Silicon tubes and aquarium pump tubes may be purchased at a pet store. Syringes may be purchased at fine grocery stores as part of a turkey injection kit, as the opening is a perfect fit for the silicon tubes.

Tim McKee | Executive Chef, La Belle Vie

Imagine Chef Tim McKee not knowing to how to properly chop vegetables or braise meat. He refers to the beginning of his culinary career as being "in way over my head". No matter, he was only working as a prep cook to pay for his college education.

Enter Jay Sparks, the D'Amico chef credited for grooming great chefs, such as Tim McKee and Isaac Becker.

McKee assumed he would eventually go back to school and get a job in his field of study, but for now he was having a lot of fun learning from Sparks. When Sparks was sent to head the kitchen at D'Amico Cucina, at the time one of only three fine dining restaurants in Minneapolis, he took McKee with him as his sous chef.

Eventually, McKee would take over his mentor's position as executive chef at the award-winning restaurant. In 1997, *Food & Wine Magazine* called McKee to tell him they named him as one of the "Best New Chefs" and it was at that point he decided that being a chef was his calling and a career in anthropology and geology would have to wait.

As the first Minnesota chef to win a James Beard Best Chef Midwest Award (the culinary equivalent to winning an Oscar), McKee has a wide breadth of cuisine under his belt. Between his own restaurants and those he is consulting chef, his menus include French Mediterranean, Spanish tapas, Italian, Caribbean barbeque, sustainable seafood and a Japanese menu to be added to that repertoire.

McKee credits much of what he has learned about cooking to Jay Sparks. He learned something else from his mentor — to serve as teacher to the next generation of chefs in the Twin Cities.

And while building a restaurant dynasty may be nice, McKee was never intent on being a big restaurateur.

The man just likes to cook.

Serves 6-8

PUTTANESCA SAUCE (makes 4 cups)

1/4 cup	extra virgin olive oil
4 tablespoons	garlic, thinly sliced
2 tablespoons	Calabrian pepper, chopped
4 tablespoons	capers
1 cup	kalamata olives, quartered lengthways
2-14 ounce cans	crushed tomatoes, drained and put in a food processor until smooth

Sweat the garlic in the extra virgin until tender, but with no color. Add the peppers, capers and olives and sauté for 30 seconds. Add the tomato sauce purée and cook for another 30 seconds.

BRAISED FENNEL & ARTICHOKES

2 cups	blended olive oil
1 cup	extra virgin olive oil
1 tablespoon	kosher salt
4 cloves	garlic, thinly sliced
2	thyme sprigs
1	bay leaf
3 ounces	white wine
2 ounces	lemon juice
1	fennel bulb
8-12	baby artichokes

Combine first 8 ingredients in stainless steel pot and heat to a simmer. Turn off heat and allow flavors to develop.

Cut the top off the fennel and remove the core. Cut the fennel into 8 pieces. Add to the braising liquid and cook on a low simmer until tender, about 10 minutes.

Trim the baby artichokes. Remove the darker green leaves, and the dark green parts around the stem, so that only the pale green parts remain. With a paring knife remove the fibrous green stem and cut in half. Immediately place in the braising mixture to prevent discoloration. Cook at a low simmer until tender, about 15 minutes.

(continued)

ASSEMBLY

	braised fennel & artichokes
	blended olive oil for sautéing
8 pieces	skate wing, roughly 5 ounces each
	kosher salt and freshly ground black pepper
	all-purpose flour, enough to lightly coat the fish
2 tablespoons	unsalted butter
2	lemon halves
24	assorted cherry tomatoes, cut in half
	puttanesca sauce

Gently heat the fennel and artichokes and keep warm.

Heat 2 large sauté pans on high and add the oil.

Season both sides of skate with salt and pepper and lightly dredge the fish in the flour. Make sure to brush off any excess flour, or it will burn.

Add the skate to the pan and continue cooking on one side until golden brown. Make sure the pan has plenty of oil and that the pan is not crowded — the pieces of fish should have enough room so they do not touch. When one side of the skate is browned and crispy, turn the fish, sauté for 1 minute and add the butter. Allow the butter to brown and continue to cook the skate until crispy. Squeeze the lemon over the fish.

Remove the fish from the pan to a platter, and discard the oil/butter. Immediately add the tomatoes and sauté for 1 minute. Add the puttanesca sauce and heat until just warm.

To serve, place a few slices of the braised fennel on a plate, spoon the tomatoes and sauce around, place the fish on top, and garnish with the braised artichokes.

Pesce Spada Sott'Olio
(Preserved Swordfish with Heirloom Tomatoes, Radishes and Pinenuts)

Serves 6-8 as a first course

OLIVE OIL POACHED SWORDFISH

2 pounds	swordfish filet, bloodline and skin removed
1/2 cup	kosher salt
1/2 cup	brown sugar
1 tablespoon	fresh thyme, chopped
2 tablespoon	fresh oregano leaves, chopped
2 tablespoon	fresh rosemary leaves, chopped
1 teaspoon	crushed red pepper
2 cloves	garlic, finely minced
	extra virgin olive oil, enough to cover fish

Mix salt, sugar, herbs, spices and garlic in a bowl until well combined. Add swordfish and toss to evenly coat. Cover with plastic and refrigerate for about 1 hour or until the fish is starting to firm up from the cure. Lightly brush away any excess cure and place in a saucepot. Cover with extra virgin olive oil enough to just cover the fish and turn heat to low. Cook over very low heat so as not to overcook the fish.

Flip the fish 5 minutes into cooking. Once the oil becomes hot to the touch, turn the heat off and cover the pot. Let the fish continue to cook for about 10 minutes or until the interior reads 140° on a thermometer. Place fish on a plate, cover with plastic and refrigerate until ready to use.

BASIL PESTO (makes 2 cups)

3 cloves	garlic
2 teaspoons	kosher salt
4 ounces	pinenuts, toasted until golden brown
2 ounces	fresh basil leaves
2 ounces	Parmesan cheese, finely grated
1 ½ cups	blended oil

Add garlic, salt and Parmesan cheese to a food processor and pulse until chopped. Add pinenuts and fresh basil and pulse until smooth. With the blender running, slowly add the oil to emulsify.

(continued)

TONNATO SAUCE (makes 2 cups)

1 clove	garlic
3/4 teaspoon	kosher salt
2	egg yolks
1/4 cup	water
2 tablespoons	fresh lemon juice
1 tablespoon	caper juice
3 tablespoons	capers
8 ounces	canned tuna, drained well
1 ½ cups	blended olive oil

Add all ingredients in a blender except oil and blend until smooth. With the blender running, slowly add the oil to emulsify.

ASSEMBLY

4	heirloom tomatoes, various varietals, cut into 1 ounce pieces
10	radishes, washed and cut in half lengthwise
	basil pesto
	tonatto sauce
	swordfish, cut into 1 ½ ounce portions
24	basil leaves, small to medium size
4	radishes, sliced paper thin on a mandolin and reserved in water, for garnish
	lemon juice for seasoning
	Maldon sea salt
	extra virgin olive oil for plating
	freshly ground black pepper

Dress tomatoes and radish halves with basil pesto, fresh lemon juice, Maldon salt and fresh black pepper. Sauce each plate with about 2 ounces of tonatto sauce. Place two swordfish pieces on tonatto and season with Maldon salt and fresh lemon juice.

Arrange radishes, tomatoes, basil leaves and radish garnish around plate. Finish with extra virgin olive oil and freshly ground black pepper.

Serves 6-8

MINT PASTA (makes 2 pounds)

1 pound	spinach leaves, cleaned
2 ounces	mint leaves
4 ounces	spinach/mint purée, very dry
3	whole eggs
4	egg yolks
4 cups	all-purpose flour

Bring 1 gallon of water to a boil. Add 1/2 cup of kosher salt, and return to a boil. Have a large stainless steel mixing bowl of ice water ready. Briefly blanch spinach and mint in the water and drain well. Immediately shock in ice water. Finely mince with a knife and place in a blender. Add only enough water to blender to allow it to combine, and purée until very smooth. If the mixture gets warm, chill immediately — heat will damage the color. Strain through a fine mesh strainer lined with cheesecloth and let drain until very dry, preferably overnight.

For the pasta, mix the mint/spinach purée together with the eggs. Make a well out of the flour on a large work surface. Add the egg mixture in the middle and carefully incorporate the eggs into the flour with a fork. Once the pasta comes together, knead for at least 10 minutes until smooth. Wrap dough with plastic wrap and let rest for at least 1 hour.

(continued)

LAMB RAGU

5 pounds	boneless lamb shoulder
	salt and freshly ground pepper, for seasoning
1/4 cup	blended oil
5 cups	onion, diced 1/4"
3 ounces	garlic, rough chopped
1 cup	red wine
2-14 ounce cans	whole peeled tomatoes, drained
1	bay leaf
1 sprig	fresh mint
1 cup	pitted kalamata olives

Trim most of the fat from the lamb (any fat thicker than a 1/8"). Cut it into 1 ½" cubes and season well with salt and freshly ground pepper. In a large braising pot, add the oil and brown the lamb. Pull the pot from the heat occasionally and let sit, off the heat, for 1-2 minutes, to allow you to scrape the fond from the bottom of the pan. This step is important because the fond enriches the braise and will scorch if it is not mixed back with the meat.

After the meat is brown and caramelized, add the onions and garlic, and continue to cook them until they are brown and caramelized. Again take the pot off of the burner to scrape up the fond. This may have to be done several times. Add the wine and cook until it has all but evaporated and the meat is starting to fry a little bit. Add the tomatoes, bay leaf, mint and olives and reduce until the sauce has thickened. Adjust the sauce for seasoning with salt. At this point the sauce should taste like the finished product, however the lamb will still be tough. Add 1 quart of water and continue cooking until reduced. Add more water as necessary until the lamb is very tender. Remove the bay and mint and cool.

ASSEMBLY

	mint pasta
	lamb ragu
	Pecorino Romano cheese, freshly grated

Roll the pasta to the thinnest setting on your pasta machine, going incrementally so as not to force the pasta through or tear. Cut pasta sheets into small rectangle shapes.

Bring 4 quarts of water to a boil and add least 2 tablespoons of kosher salt — the water should taste seasoned, not overly salty or bland.

Heat the lamb ragu with a little of the pasta water; keep warm.

Add the pasta to the water and cook for about 5 minutes, or until al dente. Toss the fazzoletti with the ragu and place in pasta bowls. Garnish with Pecorino Romano cheese.

"Food is our common ground, a universal experience."

- James Beard

Asher Miller | Executive Chef, 20.21 | Walker Art Center

Growing up in a creative New Hampshire household, with a teacher for a mother and a violin maker for a father, Chef Asher Miller started cooking in a way that might make a fun challenge in a chef competition.

Miller's first, and favorite, memory of cooking was an activity his mother called "mystery cooking." Armed with a variety of mysterious ingredients, the children would select ingredients to be cooked in a makeshift tin foil "pan".

The heat source? A candle.

Mystery cooking required the children to be creative and resourceful, traits needed to be a great chef.

With a quiet and patient demeanor, Miller inherited his mother's talent for teaching. Skillfully training and leading his team to execute consistent dishes for Wolfgang Puck's 20.21, but also servicing the Walker Art Center for private and public events is a balancing act of art, math and steady hand.

Miller was born with a desire to learn. With a bulk of his cooking experience being French-focused, the progression of the 20.21 menu has enabled Miller to expand his culinary scope.

The various art exhibits at the Walker Art Center also offer Miller creative license to prepare dishes which often display their own interpretation of the art. All of which keep diners curious and looking forward to what is to come next.

Call it Miller's own version of "mystery cooking".

CORN SOUP BASE

1/4	sweet onion, thinly sliced
4 tablespoons	butter
8 cups	cleaned corn
12 cups	chicken stock
	Szechwan peppercorn salt (2 cups szechwan peppercorns mixed with 1 cup salt), sugar and white pepper to taste

Toast peppercorns and salt together in a risotto pot until fragrant. Allow to cool and grind in a spice grinder.

Sauté sweet onion in butter until translucent. Add corn and continue to sweat on medium heat until corn has released some of its liquid. Season with salt, sugar and white pepper. Cover with chicken stock and cook until tender. Pulse in high speed blender and pass through small *china cap and again through a fine strainer.

SOUP

1 quart	corn soup base
1/2 cup	rice vinegar
1 tablespoon	white pepper
1 teaspoon	sea salt
2 tablespoons	sugar
1/4 cup	slurry (50/50 blend of cornstarch and water)
2	water chestnuts, sliced
1/4 cup	scallion nuggets (scallions chopped to ¼")
1/4 cup	**clamshell mushrooms
1/4 cup	king crab meat, picked over for shells
1/2 cup	caramelized corn (corn cut from the cob and sautéed over very high heat until brown)
1/4 cup	tofu, medium dice
1	egg (beaten and poured into a squeeze bottle)

Combine first five ingredients and add to wok. Add slurry and adjust seasoning. Add water chestnuts, scallions, mushrooms, crab, corn and tofu. Bring to a boil, then shut off wok. Drizzle egg in circles into the wok, taking care not to break up the egg.

Serve with garnishes of crispy ginger, garlic flowers, scallion rings, cilantro and sesame oil.

recipe notes

*A china cap is a conical strainer of perforated metal with much larger holes than a chinois.

**Clamshell mushrooms may be found at many Asian markets, or online at www.fromthefarm.com. Enoki or shiitake mushrooms can be substituted.

Serves 4-6

1/2 cup	bacon, diced
2 cups	Vidalia onion, diced
2	large carrots, peeled and diced ¼"
1	celery rib, diced ¼"
1	red bell pepper, diced ¼"
1 pound	Yukon gold potatoes, peeled and diced ¼"
5 cups	water or chicken stock
2	fresh thyme sprigs
3 cups	corn (6 ears), cut fresh off the cob
1 ½ cups	heavy cream
1 tablespoon	kosher salt
1 teaspoon	black pepper
2 tablespoons	chives, minced, for garnish

In an 8 quart sauce pot, over medium heat, cook the bacon, stirring frequently until crispy, approximately 5 minutes. Remove bacon to paper towels to drain.

Add onion, carrots, celery and pepper to bacon fat and cook until onion is translucent, approximately 8 minutes. Add potatoes, liquid and thyme and simmer, covered, until the potatoes are just tender, 15-20 minutes.

Add corn and cream and simmer for 10 minutes. Add salt, pepper and bacon, and finish with chives.

amuse bouche

Chef Asher Miller's father is a violin maker, and Asher himself plays violin.

Serves 2

LAMB

6	Colorado lamb chops, cleaned
3 cups	mushroom soy sauce
3 cups	mirin (sweet rice cooking wine)

Marinate the chops with the bone sticking up (do not coat) for 20 minutes. Remove from marinade.

VINAIGRETTE

1/2 cup	pickled ginger
1/2 cup	ginger vinegar
2 tablespoons	Chinese mustard paste (dry mustard bloomed in hot water, to the consistency of peanut butter)
1/4 teaspoon	sambal chili sauce
2	egg yolks
1 teaspoon	garlic, chopped
1/4 cup	roasted cashews
2 cups	cilantro leaves
1 1/4 cups	mint leaves
2 cups	peanut oil
1 teaspoon	sesame oil
1/2 tablespoon	salt
1 teaspoon	sugar

Add first six ingredients to blender, and combine until smooth. Add cashews, and continue to blend until smooth. Do not let blender get hot. (Refrigerate if needed). Add cilantro and mint, blending quickly. Add oils to herbs, and blend to emulsify. Season with salt and sugar. Vinaigrette should be speckled with herbs. Set aside.

(continued)

VEGETABLES

8 leaves	bok choy
4	baby carrots, sliced on a bias
12	sugar snap peas, cleaned, sliced on a bias
12	snow peas, cleaned, sliced on a bias
4 ounces	medium red onion, sliced
4 ounces	scallion batons (scallions cut to about 2" in length)
2 teaspoons	garlic, minced
2 teaspoons	ginger, minced
	pinch chili flakes
	salt and pepper

Season the lamb chops with salt and pepper and grill to medium-rare. Dot with butter pats while they rest.

Stir-fry the vegetables, garlic, ginger and chili flakes with canola oil in a wok until hot and just tender. Season with salt and pepper.

To plate, place vegetables in a neat pile on one side of the plate. Spoon 1 tablespoon of vinaigrette in three spots on the other side of the plate. Rest the meat of the chops on the vinaigrette, and the bones on the vegetables. Dot the top of the lamb chops with more vinaigrette.

amuse bouche

Chef Asher Miller's favorite candy is Jordan almonds.

Serves 4

3 pounds	boneless lamb (shoulder or leg), cut into cubes
1/4 cup	flour
3 teaspoons	kosher salt
2 teaspoons	ground black pepper
1/4 cup	olive oil
1	green pepper, coarsely chopped
4	red bliss potatoes, cut into quarters
2	medium yellow onions, chopped
1 cup	celery, sliced
5	carrots, sliced
1/2 teaspoon	marjoram
3	garlic cloves, crushed
2 cups	water

In a resealable bag, mix together lamb, flour, salt and pepper. Shake to coat.

In a large skillet, heat olive oil over medium-high heat. Add the lamb cubes, and sear on all sides until brown. Remove the lamb to a crock pot.

Add the vegetables, marjoram and garlic to the skillet while still hot, and let sweat for 4-5 minutes. Deglaze with a little water.

Transfer the vegetables and drippings to a crock pot. Add water, cover and cook on low 8-10 hours. Season to taste and serve.

recipe notes

If using a fatty cut of meat, chill stew after cooking, and discard the top layer of solidified fat prior to serving.

Adrienne Odom | Pastry Chef, Parasole

Growing up in the Upper West Side of New York City is the culinary careerist's dream. With places like Zabar's and Westside Market just steps from her family's home, Pastry Chef Adrienne Odom was surrounded by millions of New Yorkers who take food very seriously.

Are culinary masters born or taught? If you've ever tried any of Odom's mouth-watering desserts, you might argue that they are born.

As a self taught pastry chef, Odom intuitively draws on her childhood dining experiences and world travels to create pastries that would please diners from every corner of the earth.

Odom finds inspiration in learning what a person likes and creating a dessert that perfectly reflects their tastes. Knowing she can make people happy with the desserts she bakes provides an enormous sense of satisfaction.

The pastry chef made a name for herself at Aquavit in Minneapolis and left a favorable impression while producing desserts at La Belle Vie and Solera before returning to Aquavit in New York.

Returning to Minnesota offered Odom an opportunity to bring global flavors to the dessert plate. Working at Parasole with their varied restaurants means Odom gets to experiment with a variety of flavors to match the various cuisines.

While Odom admires and learns from pastry great Claudia Fleming for her flavor profiles and Richard Leech for his architectural approach, there is no doubt that every one of her desserts has her own creative signature on it.

EARL GREY SEMIFREDDO

24 ounces	heavy cream
	peel of half orange, zested
2 tablespoons	Earl Grey tea, heaping
	pinch of salt
5 ounces	egg yolks (approximately 7 large egg yolks)
4 ounces	sugar

Combine cream, orange peel, tea, and salt in saucepan. Heat and let steep for 15 minutes. Note: do not oversteep (the tannins will make it bitter). Strain and cool completely for at least 1 hour or overnight.

Mix egg yolks and sugar in large bowl. Heat over a water bath until mixture feels hot to the touch, stirring constantly. Remove from heat, and whip until thick and pale yellow in color.

Whip steeped mixture (infused cream) to soft peaks. Fold egg mixture into infused cream. Pour into desired molds and freeze overnight.

CITRUS ALMOND CAKE

1 pound	butter
12 ounces	powdered sugar
2 ½ ounces	all-purpose flour
6 ½ ounces	almond flour
	zest of 1 orange
	zest of half lemon
8 ounces	egg whites (approximately 12 large egg yolks)

Heat butter over low flame until it begins to foam. Remove from heat and it will continue to brown. Set aside to cool. Mix all dry ingredients, add zests, then add egg whites. Slowly mix in cooled brown butter, and let rest for 2-3 hours.

Pipe or spoon into desired pan (any flexible mold or cupcake pan will work) and bake at 350° for 12-15 minutes, until golden brown along the edges.

(continued)

SATSUMA FLUID GEL

12	*satsumas, juiced — enough for 1 cup (may substitute clementines or mandarins)
2 tablespoons	simple syrup (equal parts sugar and water, heated to create a syrup)
2/3 teaspoon	**agar agar

Bring ingredients to a boil for at least 2 minutes. Pour into container and let cool.

After mixture is cool, it will be a solid mass. Cut into small pieces, place in blender, and blend with water or additional satsuma juice until desired consistency is achieved. A thick gel works well.

Serve individual semifreddos alongside citrus almond cake, and garnish with satsuma gel.

recipe notes

*Satsuma is a Japanese citrus — very sweet, easy to peel and similar in size to a mandarin orange.
**Agar agar is a stabilizer and thickener, similar to gelatin. It may be found at many co-ops.

amuse bouche

Chef Adrienne Odom collects toys from all over the world and owns more than 1000 Matchbox cars.

Caramelized Apple Crostada

Serves 6-8

DOUGH

13 ounces	butter
11 ounces	cream cheese
	juice of half lemon
	zest of half lemon
13 ounces	all-purpose flour
1/8 teaspoon	cardamom
1/4 teaspoon	cinnamon

Cream butter and cream cheese, then add lemon juice and zest. Mix dry ingredients separately, then add to creamed mixture until just combined. Wrap in plastic wrap and chill for at least 2 hours or overnight.

PASTRY CREAM

2 cups	milk
1	cinnamon stick
1/2	vanilla bean
2 ounces	sugar
1 ¼ ounces	cornstarch
3 ounces	egg yolks

In a saucepan over medium heat, add milk, cinnamon, and vanilla bean and bring to a scald (almost boiling). Let steep for 5 minutes, then remove cinnamon stick and vanilla bean.

Combine sugar and cornstarch, and add egg yolks. Warm the milk mixture and add 1/4 cup to the egg mixture. Return to the saucepan with remaining milk. Whisk constantly until thick over medium heat — it burns easily and must be whisked constantly to avoid lumps. Boil mixture for at least 2 minutes, remove from heat, and let cool.

(continued)

FILLING

1/4 cup	sugar
6	large apples (preferably haralson, may substitute granny smith), peeled, cored and cut into 8 wedges each
1/4 cup	raisins, soaked in 4 tablespoons dark rum
	egg wash (whole egg mixed with milk)

Caramelize sugar in sauté pan with a heat proof spatula until golden brown. Add apples all at once and stir until coated with caramel mixture (this will take a few minutes). Add rum and raisins, being careful of the flame. Remove from heat and allow to cool.

Roll dough to 1/8" thickness and cut into 8" circles. Place 2-3 tablespoons of pastry cream on bottom of crust, followed by a layer of raisins, then apples. Fold dough towards the center, leaving some of the apples exposed. Brush with egg wash and additional sugar.

Bake at 375° for 12-15 minutes until golden brown.

Lenny Russo | Executive Chef, Heartland

Chef Lenny Russo was already heading up his family kitchen at the age of ten, presenting sophisticated dishes such as mussels with red sauce. The heart of the home was in the kitchen and cooking together was a family affair.

If Russo could cook for anyone, he wishes he could cook for his deceased Italian grandparents, as he is "such a better cook now." Kafka is a very close second.

A better cook he is, as proven by the status as a semi-finalist 2009 James Beard Award Best Chef Midwest. A ferocious reader, Russo's bookshelves are lined with European history books, cookbooks, botanical encyclopedias, all directly or indirectly impacting his culinary and political views on the agricultural and restaurant industries.

Russo has combined his love of cooking, botanical interest, economic history and political perspective to build his restaurant, Heartland.

Heartland Restaurant and Farm Direct Market provides Russo a forum in which to promote his philosophy that restaurants and the community can be supported by sourcing ingredients locally. The massive space is designed with a comfortable, yet sophisticated style offering homage to local farms with the barn wood adorning the walls.

The zero-waste approach of Heartland shows the respect Russo has for ingredients, as waste equals disrespect.

Although, the green movement may be a trend in the business world, in Russo's world it isn't a trend, but rather a lifestyle.

Pan-roasted Rabbit with Winter Squash-Barley Risotto

6 Servings

RISOTTO

1 quart	court-bouillon (see recipe)
3 tablespoons	whole unsalted butter, divided
1 tablespoon	grapeseed oil
1	white onion, peeled and diced 1/8"
1	carrot, peeled and diced 1/8"
2 ribs	celery, peeled and diced 1/8"
1	fennel, cored and diced 1/8"
1 clove	garlic, minced
1/2 pound	hulled barley
1 teaspoon	fine sea salt
1/2 teaspoon	black pepper, freshly ground
2 cups	roasted winter squash (see recipe)
1/4 teaspoon	nutmeg, freshly ground
1/4 teaspoon	fresh ginger, grated
1 tablespoon	fresh thyme leaves
1/8 teaspoon	ground cinnamon

Bring the court-bouillon to a slow simmer in a nonreactive pot. Meanwhile, heat 1 tablespoon of the butter and all of the oil in a shallow braising pan or sauce pan over medium-low heat. Add the vegetables, and lightly sauté until tender. Add the barley, and season with the salt and pepper. Sauté the barley with the vegetables until it begins to change color, stirring occasionally with a wooden spoon (this is called pearlizing). Once the barley is pearlized, slowly add the stock using a 4 ounce ladle. Continue to stir the barley as you add the stock, allowing the stock to become completely absorbed before adding another ladle's worth.

Repeat this process until all but 1 cup of the stock is used. The barley should be tender but not soft. Add the squash and the remaining spices, and ladle in the remaining stock. Continue to stir gently, simmering until the stock is absorbed and the squash is warmed through. Remove the pan from the heat and add the thyme. Gently stir in the remaining butter and adjust for salt and pepper if necessary. Cover the risotto and reserve.

(continued)

RABBIT

2 tablespoons	whole butter
6	hind legs of rabbit, thigh bone removed (chicken breasts may be substituted)
1 teaspoon	fine sea salt
1/2 teaspoon	black pepper, freshly ground
3 tablespoons	fresh rosemary, chopped

Heat a large frying pan over medium-high heat. Add the butter. Season the rabbit on both sides with salt, pepper and rosemary. Once the butter stops foaming, add the rabbit to the pan and brown well on both sides. Cover the pan and reduce the heat to low. Continue cooking for another 4 minutes.

TO SERVE

Divide the risotto equally among four serving bowls. Place the rabbit legs on top of the risotto so that the leg bone is standing straight up. Serve immediately.

Court-Bouillon

Makes 1 gallon

2	white onions, peeled and diced ¼"
3	carrots, peeled and diced ¼"
1/2 stalk	celery, peeled and diced ¼"
1	medium leek, cleaned and diced ¼"
1 bulb	garlic, quartered
2 tablespoons	grape seed oil
1 cup	dry white wine
1	bouquet garni (2 thyme sprigs, 2 marjoram sprigs, 3 parsley sprigs, 1 bay leaf, 5 whole allspice,
10	white peppercorns, 10 black peppercorns and 12 fennel seeds)

In a stock pot over moderate heat, sweat the vegetables in the grape seed oil until tender. Add the white wine and the bouquet garni. Fill the pot with 1 gallon of cold water, and bring it to a boil over high flame. Reduce the heat and simmer for 2 hours, skimming intermittently. Strain through a fine mesh strainer lined with moistened cheesecloth.

(continued)

Brown the onions and garlic in the duck fat in a shallow non-reactive sauce pot or brazier over medium-high heat. Add the pork and sausage. Cook for 10 minutes until the pork is well browned, and add the beans. Pour in the stock and the reserved cooking liquid. When the ragoût begins to simmer, stir in the tomatoes and the tomato paste. Add the bouquet garni, and season the ragoût with the salt and pepper. Cover the pan, and continue to simmer for 1 hour. Remove the ragoût from the heat, and chill immediately in an ice water bath.

To serve, spoon some of the ragoût into an oven safe baking crock. Top generously with fresh bread crumbs and dot the top with small knobs of rendered fat or whole unsalted butter. Bake in a 400° degree oven until the cassoulet begins to bubble. Remove and serve immediately.

Roasted Winter Squash

Makes approximately 3 cups

1	winter squash, medium (butternut, acorn, sweet dumpling, pie pumpkin) peeled and diced ¼"
1 cup	whole unsalted butter, melted
1/2 teaspoon	fine sea salt
1/4 teaspoon	black pepper, freshly ground
1/8 teaspoon	nutmeg, freshly ground
1/8 teaspoon	ginger, freshly grated
1/8 teaspoon	cinnamon

Toss the squash in the butter with the spices, and place onto a lightly oiled sheet pan. Roast the squash in a preheated 400° oven until tender (about 20 to 25 minutes). Remove the squash from the oven and allow to cool until needed.

amuse bouche

Chef Lenny Russo's grandfather was a professional boxer and won the Golden Gloves in 1929.

BEANS

2 pounds	great northern white beans, rinsed and checked for stones
1	smoked pork hock (½ lb. smoked bacon may be substituted) diced ¼"
1	sweet onion, peeled and studded with cloves
1	large carrot, peeled
1	bouquet garni (2 parsley sprigs, 2 thyme sprigs, 1 bay leaf, 2 garlic cloves and 15 black peppercorns)

Soak the beans overnight, making sure there is twice the water as there are beans by volume. Drain and place beans in a pot with the other ingredients. Add enough cold water again so that it is twice the volume of the beans. Bring the pot to a boil over high heat. Reduce the heat to a simmer, and gently cook the beans until they are tender but not splitting (about 1 ½ hours).

Drain the beans, making sure to reserve the cooking liquid for further use. Remove the vegetables and bouquet garni. Place beans on a sheet pan and allow to cool. Separate the meat from the pork hock and discard the bone. Return the meat to the beans.

RAGOÛT

2 pounds	sweet onions, peeled and diced ¼"
10 cloves	garlic
1/2 cup	rendered duck fat (rendered pork fat or whole unsalted butter may be substituted)
4 pounds	lean pork, diced ¼"
2 pounds	white wine garlic sausage (another French-style sausage or lean ham sausage may be substituted), cooked and sliced on the bias
2 pounds	cooked white beans (see above)
1/2 gallon	brown chicken or meat stock (an equal amount of reserved bean cooking liquid may be substituted)
2 cups	reserved bean cooking liquid
4	Roma tomatoes or 2 large tomatoes (must be ripe), seeded and chopped
2 tablespoons	tomato paste
1	bouquet garni (2 parsley sprigs, 2 thyme sprigs, 1 bay leaf, and 1 whole nutmeg)
1 tablespoon	sea salt
1/2 tablespoon	Tellicherry black pepper, freshly ground

Plum Catsup

Makes approximately 3 pints

9 cups	red or purple plums, medium ripe
1 ½ cups	light brown sugar, packed
1 cup	apple cider vinegar
1/2 cup	port wine
1/2 cup	dry red wine
2	shallots, chopped
2 cloves	whole garlic, chopped
2	cinnamon sticks
1 teaspoon	fresh ginger, grated
1/2 teaspoon	ground allspice
1/2 teaspoon	ground mace
1/2 teaspoon	ground nutmeg
1/2 teaspoon	ground cloves
2 teaspoons	fine sea salt
1 teaspoon	cayenne pepper
1	bay leaf

Pit the plums and place in a nonreactive sauce pot with sugar, vinegar and wine. Bring to a simmer over medium-low heat. Add the shallots and garlic. Simmer for 5 minutes and add the remaining ingredients. Continue to simmer until the sauce begins to thicken (about 20 to 25 minutes).

Remove the bay leaf and cinnamon sticks. Transfer catsup to a blender or food processor and purée until smooth. Allow the catsup to cool in the refrigerator — the natural pectin will thicken the sauce.

Catsup may be served warm, cold or at room temperature.

Honeycrisp Apple Mustard

Makes approximately 1 quart

1 cup	mustard seeds
1 cup	mustard powder
2 cups	water
3 cups	apple cider vinegar
6 tablespoons	wildflower honey
6 tablespoons	sorghum syrup (may substitute honey or maple syrup)
2 tablespoons	garlic, chopped
6 tablespoons	shallots, chopped
1 tablespoon	black pepper, freshly ground
1/2 teaspoon	ground allspice
1 teaspoon	ground cinnamon
1/4 teaspoon	ground cloves
1 teaspoon	ground mace
1 teaspoon	fine sea salt
12	honeycrisp apples, peeled and cored

Bring the water to boil in a nonreactive sauce pot. Add the mustard seeds and mustard powder. Reduce to medium heat and add the remaining ingredients except for the apples. Simmer for 10 minutes. Meanwhile, dice the apples and roast in a preheated 350° oven until soft (approximately 15 minutes). Transfer the mustard to a blender, and add the apples. Purée until smooth.

Serve apple mustard and plum catsup with assorted charcuterie.

"A cook is creative, marrying ingredients in the way a poet marries words."

- Roger Verge

Khanh Tran | Pastry Chef, Cosmos | Graves 601 Hotel

Having fled war-torn Vietnam in 1975, Pastry Chef Khanh Tran's family made their way to Minneapolis, Minnesota to join some of her extended family.

Weekend gatherings entailed cooking food, including the family meal of Bensalem (a large crepe-like pancake made of mong bean), for the growing Vietnamese community. Tran's fate to have a career in the culinary arts may have been decided when her aunt put her to work making rice for those gatherings, even before she was tall enough to reach the rice cooker.

The cooking tradition continued when Tran's parents opened one of the first Vietnamese restaurants in the Twin Cities, the Lotus. It was a risky proposition as Minnesotans were not familiar with Vietnamese cuisine as it is considerably different than the Chinese food they were used to.

After graduating from the Culinary Institute of America in New York and Ecole de Gastronomie Francaise Ritz-Escoffier in France, Tran returned to Minnesota and worked as a pastry chef for a handful of award-winning restaurants.

When Tran joined Graves 601 Hotel as the pastry chef, she found Cosmos a good backdrop for her creations. Her intricate, eye-appealing desserts rival the millions of dollars spent on the design and construction of the contemporary restaurant that employs her.

With the exacting precision of an architect and the aesthetic of an artist, it is no wonder Tran is an award-winning chef. In 2010, Tran received the honor of being named a semi-finalist for the 2009 James Beard Award for Outstanding Pastry Chef.

CARAMEL CREMEUX

75 grams	sugar
375 grams	cream, hot
6 grams	gelatine sheets
35 grams	water
1 tablespoon	salt

Add half the sugar into a heavy pot on medium heat. When sugar starts to caramelize, add remaining sugar until and cook until golden in color. Remove from heat the stir in the hot cream.

Bloom the gelatine in the water and melt over a water bath. Add the gelatine and the salt into the hot caramel. Pipe into a small flexi-mold and freeze.

CALVADOS APPLE MOUSSE

25 grams	egg yolks (approximately 1 ½ yolks)
75 grams	sugar, divided
15 grams	Calvados
10 grams	gelatine sheets
1/4 cup	water
75 grams	egg whites (2-3 egg whites)
1/2 cup	heavy cream (118 grams)
250 grams	apple purée

Combine the egg yolks, half the sugar and the Calvados in a stainless steel bowl and whip over simmering water until mixture is thick and reaches 165°. Bloom the gelatine in the water and melt over a hot water bath. Combine the gelatine into the warm yolk mixture.

Whip the egg whites with the remaining sugar to a medium peak. Whip the heavy cream to a soft peak.

Gently fold the egg whites into the yolk mixture, then fold in the whipped cream. Pipe into round flexi-mold, and insert the caramel cremeux in the center. Top with apple mousse, then top with chocolate sponge cake rounds. (Recipe follows.) Freeze.

(continued)

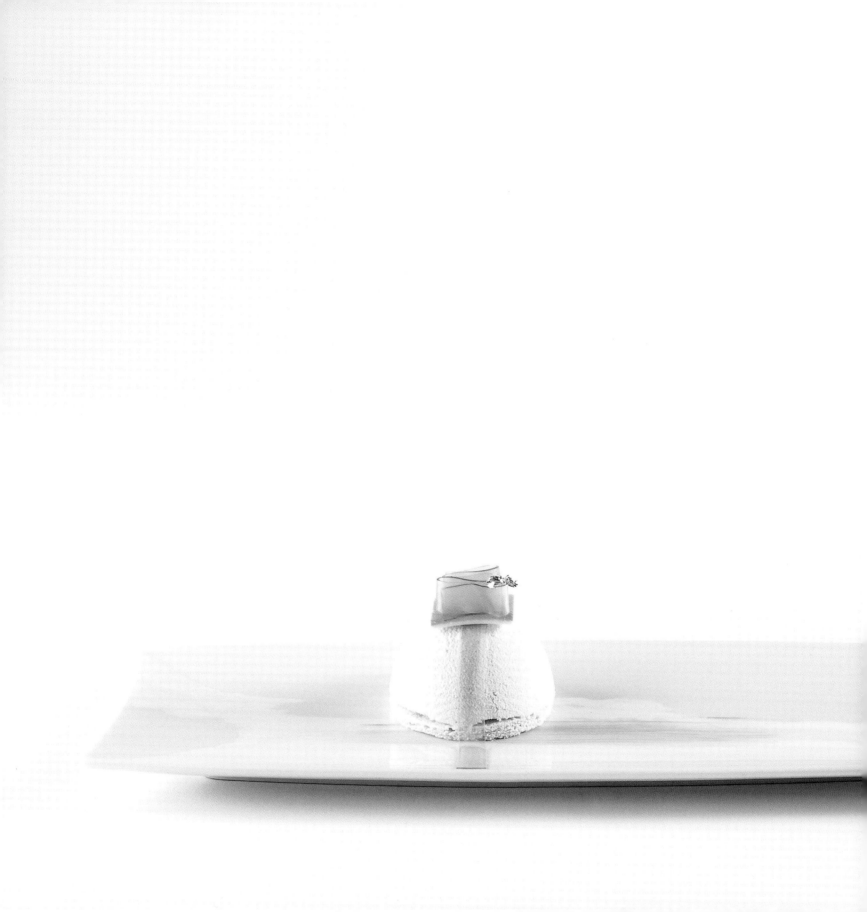

WHITE CHOCOLATE PAINT

455 grams	white chocolate
200 grams	cocoa butter

Melt chocolate and cocoa butter together. Strain, then fill a paint gun with the mixture. Unmold the apple mousse bombe, and paint the frozen mousse. (If you do not have a paint gun, simply pour the glaze over the frozen mousse.)

CALVADOS GELEE

2 cups	Calvados (French apple brandy)
6 sheets	gelatine

Bloom the gelatine and melt with the Calvados. Pour into a plastic lined square pan. Let set for 2 hours. Cut into strips and lay on top of apple bombe.

Chocolate Sponge Roulade

227 grams	egg yolks
85 grams	sugar, divided
1 teaspoon	vanilla extract
114 grams	egg whites
64 grams	all-purpose flour
22 grams	dutch process cocoa powder

Whip together the egg yolks, half the sugar and the vanilla with a whisk attachment on medium speed until thick and light in color, about 10 minutes.

Whip the egg whites and gradually add the remaining sugar while continuing to whip to a medium peak. Fold 1/3 of the whites into the yolk mixture to lighten it. Gently fold in the remaining whites.

Sift the dry ingredients together, then gradually fold into the egg mixture. Spread the batter in a sheet pan lined with parchment paper. Bake at 400° for 7-10 minutes. Cool completely and cut rounds.

Pumpkin Spice Cake

218 grams	all-purpose flour
1/8 teaspoon	ground clove
1 teaspoon	ground nutmeg
1 teaspoon	ground cinnamon
1/2 teaspoon	baking powder
1/2 teaspoon	baking soda
1/2 teaspoon	salt
228 grams	pumpkin purée
120 grams	brown sugar
100 grams	sugar
40 grams	water
100 grams	vegetable oil
1 teaspoon	vanilla extract
3	eggs (150 grams)

Sift the flour, spices, baking powder, baking soda and salt in a large bowl.

Place the pumpkin purée in a mixing bowl. Add the brown sugar and the sugar. Add the water and vegetable oil. Gradually add the eggs. Scrape bowl to combine thoroughly and add the sifted dry ingredients until well combined.

Bake at 340° for 8-10 minutes. Cool and slice.

Pumpkin Pie

At the hotel this dessert is served with nutmeg ice cream.

GRAHAM CRUST

284 grams	graham cracker crumbs
110 grams	brown sugar
170 grams	butter, melted

Combine ingredients together and press into a parchment lined half sheet pan (18" x 13"). Bake at 350° for 5-7 minutes.

PUMPKIN PIE FILLING

910 grams	pumpkin purée
2 tablespoons	corn starch
432 grams	brown sugar
2 teaspoons	ground cinnamon
2 teaspoons	ground ginger
1/2 teaspoon	ground clove
1/2 teaspoon	ground nutmeg
1 teaspoon	salt
2 cups	heavy cream (464 grams)
2/3 cup	milk (162 grams)
6	eggs (300 grams)
1 teaspoon	vanilla

In a sauce pan, heat the pumpkin purée, cornstarch, brown sugar, spices and salt. Whisk in the heavy cream and milk, and bring to barely a simmer. Remove from heat and blend until smooth, using a hand blender.

Fill crust (filling should be warm or at room temperature when filling the crust) and bake at 340° for 20-30 minutes. Cool completely and cut into a rectangle or any size you would like.

(continued)

CHANTILLY CREAM

2 cups	heavy cream
57 grams	confectioners sugar
1 tablespoon	vanilla extract

Whip the cream to very soft peaks. Add the sugar and vanilla and whip to a firm peak for piping on top of the pumpkin custard.

CARAMELIZED PUFF PASTRY

| 1 package | frozen puff pastry |
| | honey to glaze |

Place one sheet of puff pastry on top of a sheet of parchment paper, and top with another sheet of parchment. Place 2 pans on top of the second parchment paper. (A heavy pot may also be used to weigh down the pan.) Bake at 375° for 20 minutes. Check for color and rotate pan. Bake for another 20 minutes until golden in color and pastry will not puff any longer.

Remove puff pastry and glaze with a layer of honey. Place back into oven for 5 minutes. Let cool slightly and cut into desired size when warm. Place in an airtight container.

TO ASSEMBLE

Pipe the chantilly cream on top of the pumpkin custard. Top the chantilly cream with the caramelized puff pastry.

Serve immediately with vanilla ice cream.

amuse bouche

Pastry Chef Khanh Tran shows her Canadian Royal pedigreed miniature poodle in dog shows.

COFFEE CREAM

250 grams	heavy cream
250 grams	whole milk
40 grams	sugar, divided
22 grams	chicory Café du Monde coffee beans, ground
1/4 teaspoon	salt
90 grams	egg yolks (5-6 yolks)
250 grams	milk chocolate

Heat the cream and milk with half the sugar. Add the coffee grounds and steep for 10 minutes. Strain with a cheesecloth and push out the liquid. Place cream mixture back on the heat.

Temper the egg yolks and remaining sugar into the cream. (To temper, dribble the yolk mixture in a steady stream into the cream, quickly whisking the two together. This raises the temperature of the yolks gradually and cools the milk slightly.) Cook on medium to low heat to 180° or until it coats the back of a spoon. Add the milk chocolate and mix with a hand blender.

CHOCOLATE SPONGE ROULADE

227 grams	egg yolks (12-13 yolks)
85 grams	sugar, divided
1 teaspoon	vanilla extract
114 grams	egg whites
64 grams	all-purpose flour
22 grams	dutch process cocoa powder

Whip together the egg yolks, half the sugar and the vanilla with a whisk attachment on medium speed until thick and light in color, about 10 minutes.

Whip the egg whites and gradually add the remaining sugar while continuing to whip to a medium peak. Fold 1/3 of the whites into the yolk mixture to lighten it. Gently fold in the remaining whites.

Sift the dry ingredients together, then gradually fold into the egg mixture. Spread the batter in a sheet pan lined with parchment paper. Bake at 400° for 7-10 minutes. Cool completely and cut rounds to fit into a glass.

(continued)

MASCARPONE CREAM

71 grams	egg yolks (approximately 4 yolks)
85 grams	sugar
1/4 cup	sweet Marsala wine
12 grams	gelatine sheets
1/4 cup	water
227 grams	mascarpone, softened
1 cup	heavy cream, whipped to a soft peak

Combine the egg yolks, sugar, and Marsala wine in a stainless steel bowl and whip over simmering water until mixture is thick and has reached 165°.

Bloom the gelatine in the water and melt over hot water. Blend the melted gelatine into the warm egg mixture. Fold the egg mixture into the mascarpone. Fold in the whipped cream. Pipe into glass and small flexi-mold. Freeze the flexi-mold.

COFFEE JELLO

18 grams	gelatine sheets (8 sheets)
2 cups	strong chicory coffee

Bloom the gelatine in some ice cold water for 5 minutes. Squeeze out excess water and mix into the coffee. Pour mixture into a square pan and let set in the refrigerator for at least 2 hours. Cut into cubes.

TO ASSEMBLE

Place the cut chocolate sponge on top of the coffee cream. Unmold the frozen mascarpone cream and place it on top of the cake. Top the cream with the coffee jello cubes. Top glass with a coffee filter and fill with chicory coffee grounds. Add hot water into the filter to serve.

Stephen Trojahn | Executive Chef, Gastrotruck

While enjoying his job as an entry-level cook for a hotel, Chef Stephen Trojahn was not enjoying his pursuit of a traditional higher education. It was not until his boss asked him if he was planning on pursuing a career as a chef that he became aware that a culinary career was even an option.

Suddenly, his future held so many possibilities.

Starting at the ground level allowed him to learn how to cook. Rising through the ranks taught him about managing a team of chefs, all with different aspirations.

Working for the Ritz Carlton led to positions in several tropical islands, exposing him to new cuisine and ingredients with an emphasis on using fresh ingredients. After a tour of positions in Puerto Rico and Jamaica, he set his sight on a loftier goal. As executive chef at the legendary 21 Club in New York City, Trojahn caught the eye (and the palate) of culinary headhunters.

Being recruited to take over the culinary operations at a luxury hotel in Minneapolis seemed to the perfect position for Trojahn — marrying his culinary talents with his teaching while managing approach. While Minnesota seemed so far away from the tropical climates he was used to, Trojahn felt completely at home in the restaurant and hotel corporate executive chef position.

Now on his own and making Minnesota his home, Trojahn has been spending his time as a consultant to new restaurants, as well as on some projects of his own. With his food truck, Gastrotruck, and plans to open a restaurant underway, Trojahn can thank the man who innocently questioned his career path that now seems so bright.

Mustard Seed Caviar

This pairs well with fish, as a topping for deviled eggs or for seafood hors d'oeuvres.

2 ounces	olive oil
3 ½ ounces	whole mustard seeds
1/4 cup	water
1/4 cup	apple cider vinegar
1/4 teaspoon	sugar
1/2 teaspoon	kosher salt

Heat a saucepan over low heat and add oil. Stir in mustard seeds, water and vinegar and cook, covered, for 2 hours, or until tender. Drain mustard seeds. In a bowl combine mustard seeds with sugar and salt. Cool in refrigerator.

amuse bouche

Chef Stephen Trojahn was nick-named "Big Dog" by his Ritz Carlton boss, Top Chef's Kenny "Preppin' Weapon" Gilbert.

Sautéed Arctic Char, Pumpkin Seed Pesto, Turnip Purée

PUMPKIN SEED PESTO

1/2 cup	toasted pumpkin seeds
1/3 cup	Parmesan cheese, grated
3 teaspoons	lemon zest
1/2 cup	Italian parsley
1/2 cup	cilantro
2 cloves	garlic
1 teaspoon	salt
1/2 teaspoon	black pepper
2/3 cup	grape seed oil
1/3 cup	pumpkin seed oil

Place all ingredients in food processor except grape seed oil and pumpkin seed oil. Blend mixture until smooth. Pour in oils and blend for 1 minute (may be made ahead and stored in refrigerator in tightly sealed container for up to 1 week).

TURNIPS

1 pound	turnips, peeled and chopped
1 cup	whole milk
1 tablespoon	butter
1 teaspoon	salt

Place turnips and remaining ingredients in a sauce pot over medium heat, and allow to slowly simmer until turnips are soft (25 minutes). Remove turnips from liquid, reserving liquid. Place turnips in a blender with a small amount of the reserved liquid, adding more liquid until a smooth consistency is reached. Adjust seasoning to taste.

FISH

6 ounces	arctic char filet (skin on or off)
1 tablespoon	vegetable oil
	salt and pepper to taste

Heat a heavy bottom sauté pan over medium heat. Season arctic char filet with salt and pepper. Place oil in pan, then add fish filet, skin side down, and allow to cook for 3 to 4 minutes. Flip filet and allow to cook an additional 3 to 4 minutes.

TO PLATE

Spoon turnip purée on plate, place arctic char on purée and add a small amount of pesto on top of fish. Arrange additional purée around plate.

LAVENDER LOBSTER BROTH

2	lobsters, bodies and shells (reserve the meat for another use)
4 tablespoons	olive oil
2	medium onions, chopped
4	celery stalks, chopped
3	carrots, chopped
2 cloves	garlic, chopped
1	fennel bulb tops, chopped
1/2 pound	mushrooms, chopped
4 tablespoons	parsley, chopped
4	bay leaves
4-5	plum tomatoes, chopped
1/2 cup	white wine or dry sherry
2 teaspoons	dried lavender
	water
	salt

Break the lobster shells into pieces. Open the bodies and remove the gray, feathery gills. Remove the sand sac from between the eyes, and crush the bodies so they fit in a large stewpot.

Heat the olive oil in the stewpot and sauté onions, celery and carrots over medium-high heat for 3-4 minutes. Add the lobster bodies and shells and cook for another 2-3 minutes.

Add the garlic, fennel and mushrooms, mix well and cook for another 2-3 minutes. Add the parsley, bay leaves and tomatoes, then the wine or dry sherry and lavender. Mix well and cook until the alcohol largely burns off the wine, about 3-4 minutes.

Add enough water to cover ingredients by 1". Bring to a boil, then turn down to a simmer. Simmer gently for at least 90 minutes. Strain liquid, adjust seasoning and reserve warm.

(continued)

amuse bouche

Chef Stephen Trojahn has lived and worked in seven states, five different islands and one foreign country.

BRAISED FENNEL

4	small fennel bulbs
1/2 cup	white wine
3 sprigs	fresh thyme
2 cloves	garlic
1 teaspoon	coriander seeds
1 teaspoon	fennel seeds
1/2 teaspoon	crushed red pepper
2 tablespoon	lemon juice
1/2 cup	Pernod
3 tablespoons	olive oil
2 teaspoons	kosher salt
2 teaspoons	parsley

Preheat oven to 350°. Place all ingredients except parsley into a casserole with a tight-fitting lid, and bake for 30-40 minutes, or until fennel is soft and tender.

Remove from the oven, check seasonings, add the parsley and reserve warm.

WILD RICE (for crusting scallops)

1 cup	wild rice

In a heavy bottomed sauté pan heat wild rice, dry, on medium-high heat. Stir constantly until most of the rice has popped (it will smoke a little). Allow to cool, then grind in spice grinder.

SCALLOPS

1 tablespoon	olive oil
4	U-10 sea scallops
	kosher salt and black pepper to taste
1 cup	ground wild rice
4 ounces	braised fennel
3 ounces	lavender lobster broth

Heat a heavy bottomed sauté pan with olive oil on medium-high heat. Season scallops with salt and pepper and sear scallops until a caramelized brown color is achieved on one side only. Remove pan from heat and place scallops on clean plate. Dip the un-seared side of scallop in ground wild rice, and place scallops back in pan, seared side down. Place in a 350° oven for 8 minutes. Remove scallops from oven, and reserve.

To serve, place scallops on plate with fennel and pour warm lavender lobster broth on top.

"After a perfect meal we are more susceptible to the ecstasy of love than at any other time."

- Dr. Hans Bazli

Sameh Wadi | Executive Chef, Saffron

In the early 1990's, Chef Sameh Wadi's parents finished writing a cookbook. However, with the start of the Gulf War, the book was never published.

Wadi's love of food and cooking seems to be coded in his DNA. He spent months in the kitchen with his parents while they experimented with recipes for the cookbook and remembers his mother always thinking about the next meal. While eating breakfast, what would she make for lunch? While eating lunch, what would she make for dinner?

Combining his natural love for food and formal culinary instruction, Wadi offers a Middle Eastern fine dining experience at Saffron, a restaurant named after his favorite spice. His food is known for its strong Mediterranean flavor with custom mixed spices, Spice Trail by Chef Sameh Wadi.

Award-winning Saffron is a family affair. While Wadi runs the kitchen, older brother Saed runs the front of the house. And mom can be seen in the kitchen from time to time.

As of 2010, Wadi is the youngest (and the only Minnesota) chef to appear on Iron Chef America. Choosing to compete against the only original Iron Chef Masaharu Morimoto, Wadi was at a disadvantage in the mackerel challenge against the internationally known Japanese chef. While holding his own, Wadi narrowly missed winning the battle.

Nearly twenty years after his parents wrote *The Encyclopedia of Palestinian Cuisine*, Wadi has become a nationally recognized chef — as semi-finalist in 2008, 2009 and 2010 for the James Beard Award Rising Star Chef.

While Wadi is busy cooking his heart out, there is another title he'd like to add to his resume.

Publisher.

One day he hopes to publish his parent's cookbook.

Giant Beans with Dill and Lemon

BEANS

1 ½ cups	giant beans, picked over for debris and soaked in water overnight
1	onion, quartered
2	celery stalks
4 cups	vegetable stock
4 cups	water
	salt

In a large stockpot combine all ingredients except the salt. Bring to a boil, reduce heat to low and cook for 1 hour, making sure to skim the foam from the top occasionally. When the beans are cooked all the way (soft), add salt then remove from heat and cool. Reserve in liquid until ready for use.

DRESSING

1/2 cup	extra virgin olive oil
1/4 cup	lemon juice
1 cup	dill, chopped
2	medium shallots, finely diced
3 cloves	garlic, finely diced
	salt

Add all ingredients to a food processor and emulsify. Add the dressing to the drained and cool beans and refrigerate for 1 hour.

Tabbouleh Salad

2 cups	parsley, finely chopped
1/4 cup	fine bulgur wheat
1/4 cup	tomatoes, chopped
1	green onion, chopped
2 tablespoons	mint, torn
	lemon juice
	olive oil
	salt and black pepper

Soak bulgur in water for 10 minutes. Strain and reserve for 20 minutes. Fluff with a fork. Mix all ingredients together in a mixing bowl. Adjust seasoning to taste with lemon juice, olive oil, salt and pepper.

Baba Ghanoush (Eggplant Dip with Tahini)

3	eggplants, large, pricked with a fork
1	serrano chili, finely diced
2	lemons, juiced
3 cloves	garlic, mashed into a paste
1 cup	tahini
4 tablespoons	extra virgin olive oil
	salt

On a wood burning grill, cook eggplant for 30-45 minutes, until soft and smoked lightly. Wrap the eggplant in a plastic bag and place in the fridge for 20 minutes. Remove skin from eggplant and place in a strainer to drain all the juice. Place eggplant in a food processor and purée with the remaining ingredients. Adjust seasoning with salt.

Grilled Haloumi Cheese with Watermelon

8 ounces	*haloumi cheese, cut into ½" pieces
	seedless watermelon, cut into rectangles
	extra virgin olive oil
	mint leaves

Brush haloumi with a little olive oil and place on a seasoned grill. Cook for 30 seconds per side, and place on top of watermelon. Drizzle with extra virgin olive oil and sprinkle with mint leaves.

recipe notes

*Haloumi is a traditional cheese popular in the Middle East and Greece. It has a high melting point, and so may easily be fried or grilled.

amuse bouche

Chef Sameh Wadi's nickname in high school was "Johnny Two Pants".

Hummus with Spiced Lamb

HUMMUS

1 ½ cups	dried chickpeas, soaked in water overnight
1/4 cup	cooking liquid from chickpeas
2 cloves	garlic, finely grated
1 teaspoon	fresh lemon juice
1 teaspoon	sea salt
6 ounces	tahini paste
2 tablespoons	extra virgin olive oil

Drain the chickpeas and place in a medium size pot. Cover with cold water (about 2 inches above the chickpeas) and cook on medium-high heat until they become soft and break down a little, (about 1 hour). Season the chickpeas with salt and cool, reserving them in the cooking liquid.

Once completely cooled, place the chickpeas, cooking liquid, garlic, lemon juice and salt in a food processor and process until very smooth, about 4 minutes. Add the tahini and olive oil. Adjust the seasoning with more lemon and salt if desired.

SPICED LAMB

3 tablespoons	vegetable oil
1	onion, finely diced
1/2 teaspoon	*Spice Trail tagine spice
1/4 pound	freshly ground lamb, preferably from the shoulder
2 teaspoons	pine nuts, fried in oil

Heat vegetable oil in a large sauté pan on medium heat and add the onions. Reduce heat to low and cook onions for about 5 minutes. Add the spice blend, then turn heat to high. Add the lamb and cook for 5 minutes, stirring to brown lightly. Add the pine nuts and keep warm.

GARNISH

3 sprigs	fresh mint
	Spice Trail tagine spice
2 tablespoons	extra virgin olive oil

Place the hummus on a plate and top with the warm lamb mixture. Garnish with mint leaves, Spice Trail tagine spice and olive oil.

recipe notes

*Spice Trail spices are available online at www.SaffronMpls.com.

This is a modern interpretation of a classic North African dish.

STEWED CHICKEN

1 3-3 ½ pound	chicken, rinsed and cut in 4 pieces
2 teaspoons	Spice Trail ras el hanout
1	cinnamon stick
4 cloves	garlic, lightly crushed
1/4	onion, sliced
2 tablespoons	salt
3 cups	chicken stock
2 cups	water

Preheat oven to 425°.

Season the chicken with salt and ras el hanout. In a Dutch oven or a pot large enough to hold the chicken, place all items for the stew and bring to a simmer, skimming the top often. Simmer on low heat until chicken is cooked through, about 1-1 ½ hours. Strain the liquid and reserve. Discard the vegetables and shred the chicken meat, removing all bones and skin. Reduce the liquid by half and reserve.

FILLING

2 cups	*smen (may substitute clarified butter), divided
1	onion, thinly sliced
3 cloves	garlic, thinly sliced
1 teaspoon	Spice Trail ras el hanout
	salt
	shredded stewed chicken
	reserved cooking liquid
1/4 cup	Italian parsley, chopped
1/4 cup	cilantro, chopped
1-2	lemons, juiced
4	eggs, beaten
1 package	phyllo dough, thawed
1 cup	whole almonds, fried in oil and crushed
1 teaspoon	powdered sugar
1 teaspoon	ground cinnamon

(continued)

Heat 1/4 cup of smen in a sauce pan, then add onions and cook on low heat for 5 minutes. Add the garlic and Spice Trail ras el hanout, and season with salt. Add the shredded chicken and reserved cooking liquid and cook for 15-20 minutes on medium heat, or until the sauce is reduced by half.

Add the herbs and lemon juice and simmer. Stir in the eggs and let cook until the sauce congeals (remove from heat and stir continuously so the eggs do not scramble). Adjust seasoning with salt and more lemon juice to taste.

Unroll the phyllo dough, keeping it under a damp towel to prevent from drying out. Brush some of the smen on the bottom and sides of a 9" pie pan, then cover the bottom of the pan with 6 sheets of phyllo, brushing every layer with smen.

Spread the almonds in the bottom of the pan and place the chicken mixture on top. Add two sheets of phyllo brushed with smen as the top layer. Fold the overlapping phyllo and brush with more smen.

Bake in oven at 350° for 20-30 minutes or until the phyllo is golden brown.

Remove the bisteeya from oven and dust with the sugar and cinnamon.

recipe notes

*Smen is a form of preserved butter, similar to ghee. Smen is available locally at the Holy Land deli.

FRIED FISH

2	whole fish, about 1 ½-2 pounds each (striped bass, snapper, mackerel, tilapia or branzino work well. Ask fish monger to scale fish and remove innards.)
4 cloves	garlic, mashed into a paste
2	lemons, juiced
3 tablespoons	Spice Trail garam masala
	salt to taste
2 cups	all-purpose flour
1 tablespoon	Spice Trail garam masala
	oil to fry

Make a small slit in the stomach and clean fish from the inside. Wash thoroughly and pat dry. Make 4-5 ¼" cuts on both sides of the fish.

Mix garlic, lemon juice, Spice Trail garam masala and salt and marinate the fish at least 30 minutes in the refrigerator.

Combine the flour with Spice Trail Garam Masala and salt. Dust the whole fish in the spice mixture and fry in a deep fryer set at 350° for 5-8 minutes.

Remove from fryer and season with more salt.

TAHINI SAUCE

3 tablespoons	parsley, chopped
3 tablespoons	cilantro, chopped
1 clove	garlic, mashed into a paste
1	lemon, juiced
1/2	serrano chili, finely diced
1 cup	tahini
1 teaspoon	yogurt
	salt to taste

Place all ingredients in a mixing bowl and combine. Thin with water if necessary.

(continued)

TOMATO & CUCUMBER SALAD

2	heirloom tomatoes, large, cut into 8 wedges
2	Lebanese cucumbers, halved and cut into half moons
1/4	yellow onion, thinly sliced and soaked in ice water for 1 hour
1/4 cup	parsley leaves
1 teaspoon	sumac
1 teaspoon	extra virgin olive oil
	salt to taste

Place all ingredients in a mixing bowl and combine. Cool in the refrigerator for 10 minutes.

SPICY CILANTRO SAUCE

1 bunch	cilantro, chopped
4 tablespoons	sun dried tomatoes, finely chopped
1 tablespoon	cumin seed, toasted and ground
1 teaspoon	smoked paprika
1/2 teaspoon	*Aleppo chili
1	lemon, juiced
1/4 cup	extra virgin olive oil

In a food processor, combine all ingredients except the olive oil, and pulse to form a chunky paste. Slowly add the olive oil to emulsify. Cool in the refrigerator for 20 minutes.

Serve fried fish with accompaniments.

recipe notes

*Aleppo chili pepper has a moderate heat level with some fruitiness. It may be purchased online at www.thespicehouse.com.

Stewart Woodman | Executive Chef, Heidi's

To you it may just be a peanut butter cookie, but to Chef Stewart Woodman the peanut butter cookie was the beginning of his culinary career. Much of his childhood was spent at his mother's shoulder cooking in the kitchen while perfecting the peanut butter cookie.

Deciding at a young age that he wanted to play restaurateur for real when he grew up, Woodman's path to becoming chef/proprietor was filled with celebrity, drama and heartbreak.

While his parents may have fired up Woodman's interest in cooking, it was celebrity chef Eric Ripert who had the most influence. Eager to please Ripert, proprietor of the three star Michelin Le Bernardin, Woodman quickly earned a place as Ripert's sous chef. In turn, Ripert took Woodman under his wing and taught him everything he knew about cooking and running a restaurant.

After two and a half years and meeting his wife at Le Bernardin, Woodman headed west to his wife's childhood hometown of Minneapolis. Woodman quickly made a name for himself, in and out of the kitchen, and caught the attention of *Food & Wine Magazine*, who included him in 2006 Best New Chefs.

Being dismissed from two award-winning restaurants led Woodman and his wife to create the place of their dreams, Heidi's. The tiny dining room built a reputation for producing dishes with big flavors. Symbolically, the restaurant was his perfect peanut butter cookie.

Woodman achieved what he had been striving for during his culinary career when he was named a James Beard Award semi-finalist for Best Chef Midwest 2009. But his elation was short-lived as on the same day, a fire destroyed his beloved Heidi's.

Determined to reopen Heidi's, Woodman spent his hiatus from the restaurant writing his first cookbook, *Shefzilla: Conquering Haute Cuisine at Home*. Woodman discovered his love of food from his family at home. With that love in mind, no matter how sophisticated his food, there is always an element that feels like home.

Celery Bean Stew

1 cup	great northern beans, soaked overnight
4 ¼ cup	water
1	garlic head, cleaned, cloves split in half
4 tablespoons	butter
1 cup	celery, brunoise (1/8" x 1/8" dice)
1 tablespoon	salt, plus extra for seasoning

Remove beans from soaking water, discarding water. Place beans, 4 cups of water, and garlic into a medium pot and cook on medium-low heat for 1 ½ - 2 hours, until done.

Remove pot from the heat, stir in 1 tablespoon salt and let beans rest in cooking liquid until cool. Remove garlic from the beans.

Place 1/4 cup water and butter into medium saucepan and heat on medium until butter melts. Add celery and cook until tender.

Add beans and cook until beans are hot and the liquid has reduced by half. Season with salt and serve with striped bass.

amuse bouche

Chef Stewart Woodman has a degree in Peace Studies from John Abbott College in Quebec, Canada.

Serves 4

COURT-BOUILLON

3 cups	water
1/3 cup	red wine vinegar
1/4	onion
1	celery, 1 ½" dice
1	carrot, 1 ½" dice
1 ½ cloves	garlic
1 ½	bay leaves
½ teaspoon	fine ground sea salt
¾ teaspoon	black peppercorns, toasted
¾ teaspoon	coriander seeds, toasted
3	flat leaf parsley stems
1/2	thyme branch

Place the first 9 ingredients (water through coriander) into a pot and bring the mixture to a boil. Simmer 10 minutes.

Turn off heat, add parsley and thyme. Let the herbs steep for 3-5 minutes. Strain liquid, discarding solids.

ROMAINE HEARTS

12	romaine (try to find hearts with a large core)
4 tablespoons	butter
3 cups	water
2 teaspoons	salt

Peel off romaine leaves until you are left with the core (the 3-4 leaves in the center of the heart). Trim the brown from the bottom of the romaine core, then trim the sides of the romaine heart until it is smooth and conical in appearance.

Heat butter, water, and salt in a medium saucepan over low heat. Place romaine hearts in saucepan with the points up. Make sure the water/butter mixture only comes up to the bottom of the romaine leaves. Cook on lowest heat for 2-3 hours, until soft.

(continued)

BEURRE FONDUE

1 ½ tablespoons	water
8 tablespoons	butter, cold, cut into cubes
1 teaspoon	smoke powder (optional)

Bring water to a simmer in a small saucepan. Gradually whisk in butter to a creamy consistency, constantly watching heat to maintain a bare simmer; if emulsion becomes too hot, it will break down. Add smoke powder, if using.

Remove from heat and keep warm until use.

POACHED BASS

1 recipe	court-bullion (see previous recipe)
1 pound	striped bass, cleaned, cut into 4-4 ounce portions
2 cups	celery-bean stew (see previous recipe, must start the night before)
1 tablespoon	thyme leaves, picked
1/2 cup	beurre fondue (see previous recipe)
12	romaine hearts
4	flat-leaf parsley sprigs, leaves picked
1 tablespoon	bonito flakes
1 teaspoon	chile oil

TO FINISH

Place court-bouillon in a sauté pan so that the liquid will come about halfway up the side of the bass portions. Gently bring the court-bouillon to a simmer.

Place striped bass in the court-bouillon and cook 3-5 minutes on each side, until the fish is fully cooked.

Spoon celery-bean stew onto the center of 4 plates. Sprinkle thyme leaves over the stew. Coat cooked bass with beurre fondue and place on top of the celery-bean stew in the center of the plate. Place 3 romaine hearts on each plate around the striped bass. Garnish the striped bass with bonito flakes.

Garnish plate with parsley leaves and chile oil.

amuse bouche

Chef Stewart Woodman once cooked for Julia Child, while he was Union Square Café.

"Cooking is like love. It should be entered into with abandon
or not at all."

- Harriet Van Horne

Diane Yang | Executive Pastry Chef Chef, La Belle Vie

Soon after Executive Pastry Chef Diane Yang's parents landed in America, she was born.

As a first generation American, Yang strikes a fine balance between her roles as traditional Hmong wife and mother and executive pastry chef consistently introducing contemporary plated and fresh tasting desserts for the highly lauded restaurants, La Belle Vie and Solera.

A formal culinary education from Le Cordon Bleu and several years at La Belle Vie and Solera have added up to a sophistication that belies Yang's age. Not yet thirty, Yang may have a quiet way about her, but she throws a powerful culinary punch with her creations. Despite rarely emerging from the kitchen, her desserts are drawing a lot of attention.

While Yang mostly cooks savories, not sweets, at home, she focuses on bringing out the natural flavors of the ingredients regardless of what she is preparing. Her modern interpretation of classic desserts with good, old-fashioned baking skills complements the menu at the award-winning restaurant.

The ease in which she works in the kitchen exemplifies that she has earned respect of her colleagues.

Impressive when one of her colleagues (and boss) is James Beard Award winning Tim McKee.

This is a favorite recipe of mine. This recipe may be used for breakfast, lunch, a snack or dessert! It's so versatile. For breakfast you can pipe apricot, raspberry, strawberry or any kind of jam you love right into the center of the batter before baking. For lunch, you can just bake them and dust the tops with powder sugar. (This recipe can also be turned into cupcakes). For dessert, macerate some fresh berries and insert into the center before baking, or make upside down berry cakes. Serve with your choice of ice cream and you have a plated dessert.

Be careful not to overmix the batter, which will cause the cakes to be very dense and not fluffy.

8 ounces	cream cheese, room temperature
4 ounces	butter, room temperature
8 ounces	sugar
2	eggs
14 ounces	all-purpose flour
1 teaspoon	baking powder
1/2 teaspoon	baking soda
1/2 teaspoon	salt
1/4 cup	milk
1/2 teaspoon	vanilla extract

Cream the cream cheese, butter, and sugar until smooth (remember to stop and scrape the bowl often). Add eggs, one at a time (remember to stop and scrape). Do not overmix.

Sift all dry ingredients.

Mix the milk and vanilla together, and alternate adding the flour and milk mixture into the egg batter. DO NOT OVERMIX! Mixer should be on slow speed.

Bake at 350° until the top of the cake springs back when touched.

(continued)

HARALSON APPLE BALLS

6	haralson apples, peeled and balled (with melon baller)
1 cup	water
2 cups	white wine
2 tablespoon	lemon juice
8 ounces	butter
pinch	salt
12 ounces	sugar

Place all ingredients in a stainless steel pot and bring it to a simmer. Shut off and immediately place in refrigerator to chill.

OLIVE OIL SYRUP

2	egg yolks
250 grams	corn syrup
pinch	salt
225 grams	olive oil (preferably a sweeter, floral extra virgin olive oil)

Place the yolks in a food processor and begin processing. Meanwhile, place corn syrup and salt in a pot and heat mixture to a boil. Once a boil is reached, add the syrup slowly into the running yolks, and allow to process for 5 minutes.

Slowly drizzle the oil into the syrup mixture, and set aside.

APPLE CIDER SHERBET

4	haralson apples, diced with skin on
1 ¼ cups	sugar
1 cup	water
1/8 teaspoon	cinnamon
1 tablespoon	lemon juice

Place all ingredients in a stainless steel pot to boil. When apples are tender, remove from heat and chill immediately.

Once mixture has chilled, place in blender and blend thoroughly. Strain through a chinois and transfer to an ice cream maker, processing according to manufacturers' instructions.

Serve cream cheese cake with haralson apple balls and apple cider sherbet, and drizzle with olive oil syrup.

CHOCOLATE CINNAMON CUSTARD

300 grams	butter
195 grams	dark chocolate chips
4	eggs
135 grams	sugar
1 teaspoon	ground cinnamon
pinch	salt

Preheat oven to 325°.

Melt butter and chocolate over a double broiler. When melted, remove from heat and lightly whisk in eggs, sugar, cinnamon, and salt.

Pour into a 9" cake pan and bake in water bath for 20 minutes. Custard should be slightly firm to the touch.

GRAHAM CRACKER ICE CREAM

4 cups	half & half
6 ounces	sugar
8 ounces	yolks
1	vanilla bean, scraped
	graham crackers, crushed

Scald half & half, then temper in sugar and yolk mixture. (Add a small amount of half & half to yolk mixture, whisking to incorporate and warm the eggs — this will ensure you don't end up with scrambled eggs). Add remaining half & half. Whisk until slightly thicken and cool over ice bath.

Add mixture to an ice cream maker and freeze according to the manufacturer's instructions.

Fold in crushed graham cracker crumbs and freeze until firm, at approximately 2 hours.

(continued)

MAPLE MARSHMALLOW

2	egg whites
1 ½ teaspoons	powder gelatin
pinch	salt
3 ounces	granulated maple sugar
1 ounce	corn syrup
1 ounce	water

Place egg whites, gelatin and salt in stand mixer and process on medium speed to a soft peak.

Place sugar, syrup, and water in a stainless steel pot and heat to 240°.

Slowly pour the sugar mixture into soft peak egg whites and beat for 2 minutes.

Spray desired molds with pan spray and pipe marshmallow mixture into mold, working quickly. Let set for 2 hours.

Serve chocolate cinnamon custard with graham cracker ice cream and maple marshmallow, and enjoy.

amuse bouche

Pastry Chef Diane Yang is the first child in her family born on American soil.

Agar agar – a stabilizer and thickener, similar to a gelatin.

Amuse bouche – French term literally translated, "mouth amuser"; a single, bite-size hors d'oeuvre not ordered from a menu by patrons, but, when served, done so according to the chef's discretion alone. These are served as an excitement of taste buds both to prepare the guest for the meal and to offer a preview into the chef's approach to cooking.

Blanch – a cooking term that describes the cooking a vegetable or fruit, where it is plunged into boiling water, removed after a brief, timed interval, and finally plunged into iced water or placed under cold running water (shocked) to halt the cooking process.

Braise – a cooking method combining use of both moist and dry heat; typically food is first seared at a high temperature and then finished in a covered pot with a variable amount of liquid.

Cassoulet – a rich, slow-cooked bean casserole originating in the south of France.

Chef de cuisine – French term for a person who is in charge of all things related to the kitchen which usually includes menu creation; management of entire kitchen staff; inventory; and plating design.

Chiffonade – "chiffon" is French for "rag" referring to the fabric-like strips; the cooking technique in which herbs or leafy green vegetables (such as spinach and basil) are cut into long, thin strips.

Chinois – conical sieve with an extremely fine mesh, used to strain custards, purees, soups and sauces to produce a very smooth texture.

Court-bouillon – a vegetable broth or fish stock prepared with herbs, salted water and white wine, used for poaching fish.

Cryovacking – an industry term for a cooking technique in which food is placed in a plastic bag, vacuum-packed, and then cooked slowly in warm water. The pressure of the packing process is used to infuse flavors into ingredients.

Deglaze – a technique adding wine or other liquid to a pan in which meat has been roasted or sautéed, to make a sauce incorporating the cooking juices.

Emulsify – to disperse, as an oil, in an emulsion; to convert two or more immiscible liquids into an emulsion.

Executive chef – English term for a person is in charge of all things related to the kitchen which usually includes menu creation; management of entire kitchen staff; inventory; and plating design.

Farro – food product consisting of the grains of certain wheat species in whole form.

Foie Gras – duck or goose liver.

Haloumi – a traditional cheese popular in the Middle East and Greece. It has a high melting point, and so ma easily be fried or grilled.

Julienne – cut into thin strips or small, matchlike pieces.

Langoustine – a small edible lobster of European seas having long slender claw.

Mince – to cut or chop into very small pieces.

Molecular Gastronomy – practiced by both scientists and food professionals who study the physical and chemical processes that occur while cooking. Molecular gastronomy seeks to investigate and explain the chemical reasons behind the transformation of ingredients during the cooking process.

Satsuma – a Japanese citrus that is very sweet, easy to peel and similar in size to a mandarin orange.

Sauté – a method of cooking that uses a small amount of fat in a shallow pan over relatively high heat.

Shock – A technique used primarily with vegetables, that "shocks" the food item by exposing it to ice water after it has been blanched.

Simmer – to cook at or just below the boiling point.

Smen – a form of preserved butter, similar to ghee.

Sous chef – second in command and direct assistant of the Executive Chef or Chef de Cuisine.

Terrine – refers to a vessel for cooking a forcemeat loaf; refers to a forcemeat similar to pate.

Zest – citrus peel, typically orange or lemon, used for flavoring.